MASK MAKING

Creative Methods and Techniques

by

MATTHEW BARANSKI, ED.D.

Author and Educator

Illustrated by the author

Library of Congress Catalog Card Number 54-12542

DEDICATION

TO MY MOTHER AND DAD

TABLE OF CONTENTS

ACKNOWLEDGMENTS

The author wishes to express his sincere thanks to the Buffalo Board of Education for the use of the school facilities, the Director of Art Education and the many kind and helpful teachers. To Dr. Burvil H. Glenn of the School of Education of the University of Buffalo for his valuable suggestions and for the use of the library facilities. To the Buffalo Museum of Science for the examples of masks used in the appendix. To my brother, Lucien, for technical information relative to printing and reproduction. To Eugene Lorence, Gerald Ruth, Dante Terrana and Hal Been for generous help with photography.

Many adults, as well as children, have taken part in making this book a reality . . . but especially, the children. We take this opportunity to express our sincere thanks for their cooperation. We wish we could include photographs of all the children who worked on the masks. However, the children who do appear in this book are some of those who actually worked on the masks. They are: Barbara Breidenstein, Frontispiece; Michael Baranski, opp. p. 1, pp. 2 and 3; Mary Seidel, pp. 5, 8 and 9; Philip Swiantek, pp. 10, 12 and 13; Dolores DelPrince, Anthony Queeno and Elaine Slominski, p. 20; Melvin Steinhart, pp. 28, 29 and 50; Jeanine Dziak, p. 36; Dorothy Stearns, pp. 37 and 43; Lois Barrow, pp. 48 and 49; John Brodziak, pp. 50 and 52; Betty Walkowski, p. 54; Geraldine Augino, pp. 55, 57, 60 and 61; Stephanie Baranski and Felicia Baranski, p. 66; Joe Louis Gladden, pp. 74 and 75; Sylvia Baranski and Tanny Jurgens, p. 95.

Last, but not least, to my dear wife, Rita, whose inspiration, untiring efforts and devotion are reflected in every phase of the book.

M. B.

INTRODUCTION

This book is an outgrowth of experiences in which many people have taken part. It is written for art educators, beginning or advanced craftsmen, hobbyists, group counselors, guidance personnel, school administrators and others wishing a source of inspiration, processes and techniques for making masks creatively and with a wide variety of media.

There are masks for all ages, beginning with the first grader in the elementary grades and include junior and senior high school pupils as well as adult education groups. For the mask making activities included in this book, only simple tools and inexpensive and easily acquired materials are needed; and the methods and suggestions for making them have been tried and tested.

A wide variety of materials and techniques are employed as well as many different structural approaches to making a mask, such as the use of rubber balloons, fiberboard three-dimensional forms, tin foil, masking tape, corrugated cardboard forms, plasticine forms, chicken wire, plaster molds, liquid rubber molds and others. Each chapter is clearly illustrated with photographs and pen and ink sketches of processes and finished pieces. The book is written in a simple, direct style and is the outgrowth of real experiences in a classroom.

Because mask making correlates many art activities, it is of value to people interested in modeling and sculpture, designing, cartooning, drawing and painting. This book is of value to teachers and pupils not only as a reference book and teaching aid for the classroom but also for leisure-time activities for craftsmen and hobbyists. Camp counselors will find it acquaints them with interesting and fascinating things which youngsters find a delight in doing. Guidance personnel will find it of value to better acquaint them with art activities. School administrators will enjoy reading about children at work and may better visualize the possibilities of using masks to further public relations. Therapists will find this subject offers a new outlet of help and inspiration. Throughout the book the emphasis is placed on the worth of the individual, his interests and abilities, rather than on fixed principles, rules and regulations, or technical skills. Creativeness and originality are the keynote.

And now, turn the pages of this book for new and exciting experiences!

M. B.

CHAPTER ONE

PAPER BAG MASKS

Little children can have more fun with a piece of paper than with many expensive toys. They like the way paper behaves and the crumpling and rustling sound of paper has no end of fascination for the youngster. Paper bags have a good sound to them. They are tough, can take a lot of punishment and come in a large assortment of sizes, colors and textures. Some bags even have small windows in them for the purpose of displaying their contents. To some imaginative youngster this might suggest a Martian helmet. Most paper bags take crayon and paint well and may be easily cut with blunt-point scissors.

Plain, brown bags, size No. 20, the kind folks usually bring their groceries home in, are good all-around bags with which to make masks. The first step in making a paper bag mask is to have the youngster select a bag that will fit over his head comfortably. Next, have him place his hands over the bag that is covering his face to locate where to cut the openings through which he can look comfortably, as shown in Photograph 1 on page 2. By pressing gently over the bag around the nose and mouth, the crumpled area will give enough evidence where features may be cut out or painted to correspond to those of the wearer.

Now, remove the paper bag from the head, lay it flat and draw in the features as shown in Photograph II on page 2. To get a start when using blunt-point scissors, make a small fold across the line you have sketched, make a small cut, open and insert your scissors into the opening and cut along the line as shown in Photograph III on page 2. When you have finished cutting along the lines, fold the eyes and lips on the dotted lines. The openings in your mask are completed and correspond to the features of the individual who is making the mask. The shape of the openings may

1

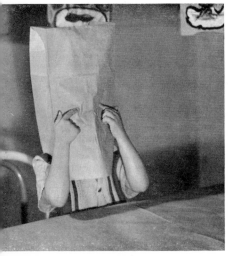

Photograph I

Locating the features

Photograph III

Folding and cutting along the line to form the eyes

Photograph II

Drawing in the features

Photograph IV
Elaborating the features with charcoal

Photograph V
Painting the mask

Photograph VI
A new experience!

3

vary to satisfy individual expression. This is only one suggestion as to how to make openings in the mask.

After the openings are cut and folded, you are ready to continue with the fun of mask making. Please keep in mind that small openings for the features are better than large ones for, whereas small openings carry with them the element of mystery, large, cutout openings spoil the effectiveness of the mask and at best look like empty, meaningless holes. Even though the slots and openings are small, the features may be elaborated by first drawing them with a piece of charcoal or pencil as shown in Photograph IV on page 3. Small openings are also better in that more effective expressions can be created by using paint or crayon. The openings themselves serve to enable the wearer to look through the mask. It is surprising to discover how small the openings need be to see clearly and unobstructedly, providing that they are properly located. Figure 1 below shows how the muscles of the face change the shape of the features to show different emotions.

Photograph V on page 3 shows the pupil painting the mask with tempera colors. Crayons may be used as an excellent substitute for paint. Photograph VI on page 3 shows a completed mask worn by the young artist.

These simple paper bag masks may be elaborated in many different ways, depending upon the creative ability, talents and ambitions of the pupils and the projects undertaken by the group.

AFRAID   SERIOUS   SURPRISE   CONCERN   PAIN

GOOD   ANGRY

BAD   HAPPY   PLEASURE   GRIEF   HATE

Figure 1

CHAPTER TWO

COLORED CONSTRUCTION PAPER MASKS

The many bright colors in which construction paper comes is a real attraction to the youngsters in the third and fourth grades as well as in other grades. Add a pencil, a pair of scissors and some transparent Scotch tape and this becomes a challenge to any youngster. Mention the magic word "mask," and you have started the wheels of imagination going at high speed.

Making masks out of colored construction paper is easily and quickly accomplished. The first step is to make a basic pattern. This is simply done by placing a piece of twelve- by eighteen-inch construction paper over the face and having another person draw a pencil line on the paper, following the jaw and around the ear. The top line along the forehead should be approximately two and one-half inches above the hairline at the center and should curve gently toward the hairline at the temples, and then follow parallel with the lower line around the head about two and one-quarter inches above the ears. The contours of the pattern may be seen in Photograph I on page 8.

Next, have the person locate the eyes, nose and mouth with his fingers while you mark them in with a pencil. Once the contours of the pattern and features are marked out, fold the sheet in half. Carefully sketch in the eyes, nose and mouth. By studying Photograph I, you will see that only the lower half of the eye is drawn and cut and is then bent upward. The same holds true for the lip. The nose is cut only about three-quarters of the way up and is then also bent upward.

A V-shaped slot is cut at the top of the mask, extending downward about two and one-half inches. Slightly smaller slots are cut at the temples and chin as shown in

Photograph I. The dark lines indicate where the paper is to be overlapped.

When the pattern is completed, select another piece of construction paper, twelve by eighteen inches. The color will be determined by the kind of individual you are going to portray. If, for example, you are planning to make an Indian, a dark red would be appropriate, whereas yellow would be fine for an Oriental. Yellow-orange or light-orange would be used for people with "white" skins.

Now fold your paper in half, place it into your pattern and trace half of your mask as shown in Photograph II on page 8. Next, with a pair of scissors cut along the contour lines of the mask and then along the lines of the features. When cutting along the lines for the eyes, make another fold down the center of the eye and in this way both eyes will be cut at the same time as shown in Photograph III on page 8.

Open your mask out flat, turn up the eyes, nose and lower lip which now becomes the upper part of the lip, and you are ready to shape your mask in such a way that it will fit comfortably over your face. This is accomplished by overlapping your mask at the V-shaped slots. In Photograph IV on page 8, we see the pupil overlapping the mask at the V-shaped slot at the forehead and keeping it in place with a piece of transparent Scotch tape one-half inch wide and about an inch long. The overlap at the forehead is approximately an inch and one-half at the top. The overlap at the temples and chin is about half an inch. The band of paper which goes around the head will not be long enough so you will have to add to it by attaching another piece of paper to it with transparent Scotch tape. Now your basic mask is complete.

Photograph V on page 9 shows the pupil curling, which simply means pressing a strip of paper between the thumb and the sharp edge of the scissors a couple of times to make it curl. Curling is effectively used for making hair arrangements, eyelashes, mustaches and sideburns. When making the hair for the mask shown in Photograph VI on page 9, the pupil first fastened a long piece of paper approximately five inches wide and eighteen inches long to the forehead and then to the back of the headband. Both the front and back ends of this piece of paper were cut into strips approximately one-half inch wide and four inches long and then curled. Two more similar pieces were used to form the hair at the sides of the head. Eyebrows and eyelashes were also held in place with transparent Scotch tape. When the mask was completed it was easily slipped over the head and worn by the pupil as shown in Photograph VI.

Photographs VII and VIII on page 9 show other variations of the basic head used to form different types.

Not only are these masks inexpensive, quickly and easily made, but they are light, comfortable to wear and if held securely together with Scotch tape, are quite durable. Another advantage of this type of mask is that the features may be easily and quickly placed in different ways to create new types and different emotional expressions.

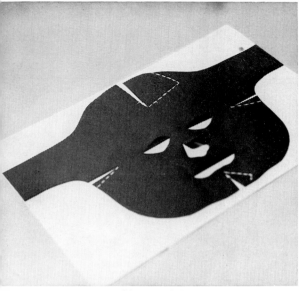

Photograph I

Basic pattern

Photograph II

Tracing the pattern

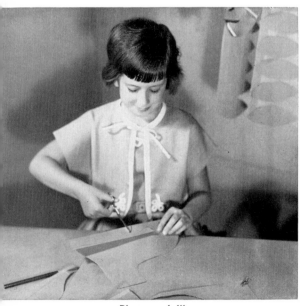

Photograph III

Cutting along the feature lines

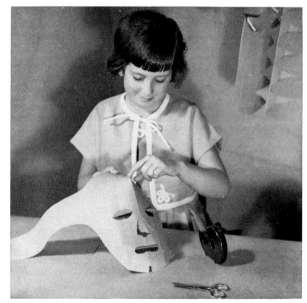

Photograph IV

Overlapping and fastening with transparent tape

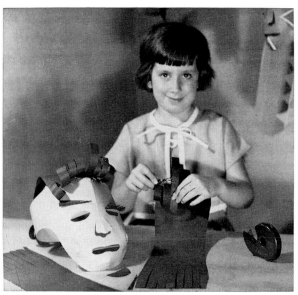

Photograph V

Fastening on the details and curling

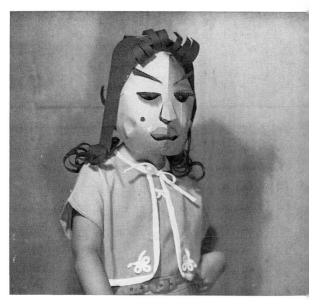

Photograph VI

What a change!

Photograph VII

Another example

Photograph VIII

Still another mask

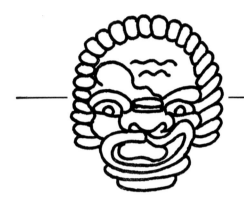

CHAPTER THREE

BALLOON MASKS

Children in the lower and intermediate grades like to work with large, simple forms and shapes and get things done quickly. There is a freshness and directness of expression that is unfortunately often lost as the pupils move on toward junior and senior high school.

Using balloons on which to form three-dimensional masks has many advantages over using crumpled newspapers and other materials as a base over which a mask is made. In the first place, it is less messy than using wads of paper since less paper and paste is used; it is a quicker and more flexible method and the mask dries more rapidly; the completed product can turn out to be more symmetrical and have a more finished-like appearance; it may be carried out in a more orderly, step-by-step method; balloons are inexpensive, come in many shapes and sizes and may be used over and over again. Besides the balloons, the other materials needed are school paste, several sheets of newspaper, paper toweling or colored comic papers and rubber bands.

Let us take a peek at a fifth-grader at work on a mask, using balloons as a base to work over, and follow him step by step.

To begin with, select various sizes of balloons; this is important since a variety of sizes and shapes adds interest. Your largest balloon should be used for the head and when inflated it should be at least two inches larger all around than the head of the wearer. After your balloon is blown up to the desired size, as shown in Photograph I on page 12, give the appendix several twists, fold over in two and hold it securely in place with a rubber band. A long, narrow balloon may be selected for the nose, and

11

Photograph I
Take a deep breath and blow hard

Photograph II
Let's put on the ears

Photograph III
Like pulling a rabbit out of a hat

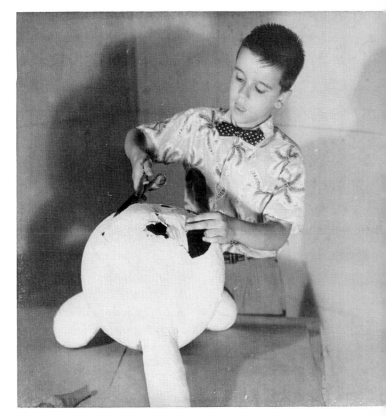

Photograph IV

Cut out to make room for the head

Photograph V

Sketching in the details

Photograph VI

At last—the finishing touch

13

two smaller, rounder ones used for the ears as shown in Photograph II on page 12. This photograph also shows how the large balloon is held in position by placing it in a pan. A bowl, small basket or a small, corrugated box might also prove to be helpful holders. Place the balloon in the holder so that the appendix points toward you. Now, tear four strips of newspaper, approximately six inches long and one and one-half inches wide and apply paste to one side of the paper. When these strips are ready, pick up the long, narrow balloon which is to be used for the nose and place it so the appendix touches the large balloon in the approximate center. Take each of the four strips of newspaper with paste and attach the nose to the head. After a few minutes, when the strips have dried, turn the large balloon so that the appendix touches the bottom of your holder and begin to attach the ears on top of the head, one on each side, in much the same manner as you attached the nose to the head. Photograph II shows the nose balloon already attached and the ear balloon being fastened to the top of the large head balloon.

Now you are ready to cover all the balloons with your first layer of newspaper strips. The strips may be torn to any size but strips six inches long and about one and one-half to two inches in width are recommended. Apply the paste evenly on one side of the strip and place over the balloon with the pasted surface up, the dry side of the paper touching the balloon. This will prevent the paper from sticking to the balloon and makes it easier to deflate and remove the balloon. Overlap the first piece of pasted paper with the next one by about one-half an inch. Keep overlapping the strips of paper, paste up, until the surfaces of the balloons are covered up.

The second layer of paper may be colored comic paper or paper toweling. Selecting a different colored or textured paper will aid you in making sure that you have covered your mask completely. This time, paste your strips of paper with the paste side down and run your fingers over it so that the paper is spread out smoothly and securely fastened to the paper underneath. When the second layer of paper is pasted completely around the mask, begin pasting the third layer which should be a different color or texture than the second layer.

You will observe that regular school paste dries quite rapidly so that by the time you finish applying the layer of paper around your mask, the paper at the place where you started has dried enough to receive the next layer of paper. Wheat paste or flour and water may be used as a paste if no school paste is available; however, both of these are more on the wet side and take longer for drying. At least four layers of paper are necessary to make a strong, durable lightweight head mask.

Since the surface of the balloons over which the paper has been pasted is smooth and even, the paper, if put on carefully, will also dry smoothly and evenly so that no sanding will be required. When you have finished applying your fourth layer of paper, your mask will look similar to the one in Photograph III on page 12.

Allow the mask to dry thoroughly in a well-ventilated room overnight before deflating the balloons. To deflate, simply remove the rubber band from the appendix of the large balloon and let the air out and pull the balloon out as shown in Photograph III. With a pair of scissors, cut out a large enough opening at the base of your mask to allow the mask to be placed over your head. See Photograph IV on page 13. When this is done, put your hand into the mask and remove the rubber bands from the appendices of the balloons which were used for the nose and ears, deflate and pull out gently. When this is accomplished, take a piece of wire and make a hoop the same size as the opening which you have cut out. Now, attach the wire to the mask with strips of paper approximately one-half inch wide and two inches long. The wire will add strength and keep the mask in shape. If no wire is available, strips of paper may be pasted around the opening to reinforce it although this is not quite as effective.

Photograph V on page 13 shows the pupil sketching in the features with a piece of charcoal. If this is not available, a soft pencil will do. After the features are sketched in, the mask is painted. In Photograph VI on page 13 we see the pupil painting the mask with show-card color paints. The mask may be waterproofed by putting shellac over the show-card colors. Another way to paint the mask would be to shellac the mask inside and out and then paint it with oil colors if these are available.

The photograph on page 10 shows the pupil wearing the completed mask which he plans to use for Halloween.

CHAPTER FOUR

PAPIER-MÂCHÉ MASKS

Papier-mâché is one of the simplest vehicles used in mask making. It is used in industry for window display models, for inexpensive toys and in many other ways. It is also used for Halloween masks, puppet heads and wall masks for decorative purposes.

The materials used in papier-mâché are always available and cost practically nothing. Papier-mâché lends itself to experimentation and to application in many areas of learning. Class experimentation with mashed paper has shown that it is simple to prepare, easily worked and can take considerable abuse when dry. It will not crack, chip or peel and can be worked very much like wood. Now, let's get to work.

The first operation is to collect some old newspapers; rough pulp paper used in cheap magazines is also excellent. Avoid smooth-surfaced papers and papers with color reproductions. If you live in a city that publishes a newspaper, it might be possible for you to collect rolls of leftover, unprinted paper. One thirty-two page newspaper will be enough to make a mask equal in size to a normal adult head.

Tear the paper into small pieces, the smaller the better. Place the torn paper in a pail of warm water to soak overnight. This is to soften and break down the paper. To hasten the breaking-down process, and for more finished and detailed modeling, the mixture of paper and water may be boiled for two or three hours. The pupil must take every precaution, either in the classroom or at home, if the boiling process is used. Although the pupil may be eager to start the actual modeling, he must remember that boiling water is not recommended as a skin lotion.

After the paper has been broken down and becomes a pulp, either by soaking or boiling, strain off the excess water, being careful not to clog the sink drain. A sug-

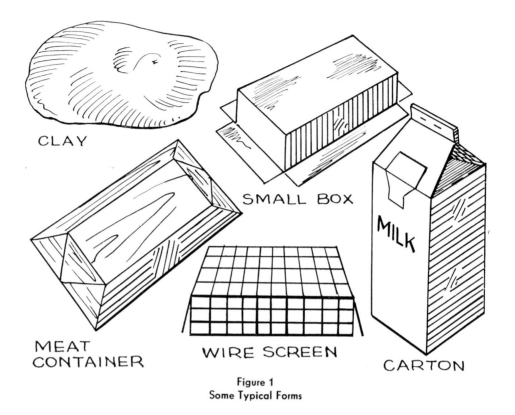

CLAY

SMALL BOX

MILK

MEAT
CONTAINER

WIRE SCREEN

CARTON

Figure 1
Some Typical Forms

gested process is to pour the wet pulp into a cloth bag and squeeze out the excess water. Then, sprinkle about one-half cup of flour or wheat paste over the paper and knead it until the paper bits become a fine, smooth, workable mash. If the boiling process has been used, any printers' ink on the paper will be evenly distributed and thoroughly mixed in the mash, tending to color it. The mash will then dry with an even, gray tone with a texture similar to concrete or stone, as shown in the photograph on page 16. Photograph I on page 19 shows the materials and equipment used in the preparation of the mash.

The mash is now ready for use. The next phase of the operation has to do with the preparation of the form on which the mask or any other object is going to be modeled. This may be prepared while the papier-mâché is soaking or boiling.

Several kinds of materials, as shown in Figure 1 on page 18 have been used for forms; for example: a lump of clay; a small box covered with wax paper; a two-pound or five-pound tin or wooden meat container as is used in butcher shops; bent wire screen, one-quarter inch mesh; milk carton.

Materials and equipment used in making papier-mâché

Photograph I

Technique used in shaping

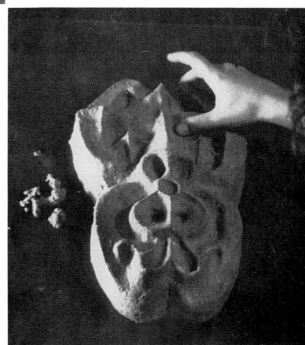

Photograph II

The meat container and the bent wire screen have been used most successfully; the meat container as a timesaver, and the wire screen to make for quick drying of the mash.

It is advisable to cover the table or drawing board with regular household wax paper before beginning to model so that the water will not damage the table or drawing board, and cleaning up will be easier. This will also make for easier handling of the finished product. Place the form on the wax paper. Take a handful of mash and begin modeling the basic shapes of the face right over the form, pressing firmly and developing large, simplified shapes into smaller, more accurate planes by adding or cutting away the mash, working toward the development of the final effect.

Although preliminary sketches, to help form some concept of the design, are an aid, they are not necessary; some of the best masks have been made when the pupil worked directly and freely with his hands to form the design which best pleased him. Photograph II on page 19 shows the techniques used in shaping. In many instances, pupils shaped and reshaped their designs for the fun of working with the material. Working with this material stimulates the imagination and motivates a child to create, which can be noted in the photograph on opposite page.

Modeling the face is an interesting process and pupils should be encouraged to experiment and get acquainted with the material before finishing their project. Since this is a slow-drying, plastic material, it allows for changes on the following day, if necessary.

If the mash has been well worked out, a surprisingly fine finish of varied textures with very good detail can be obtained. A knife, pencil or any other common flat or pointed object will aid in carrying out details.

Drying is the slowest process of all and normally takes about a week. Some methods which have proven successful in speeding up drying are: using one-quarter inch screen for forms; removing wax paper and carefully sliding mask on a window screen in a horizontal position to allow air to circulate and dry out the inside of mask; baking mask in an oven; turning mask over when the top part is dry, then removing wax paper and form to allow the inside of the mask to dry; placing mask in a well-ventilated room or out of doors in the sun.

The finished dry mask can be sandpapered, carved, bored with holes for fasteners, and painted. However, the best results are obtained when good workmanship is used in modeling and the mask is left to dry without further elaboration or finishing. Pupils should be encouraged to work for a simple, direct result. Good craftsmanship will dispose of the need for patching and "covering up."

Modeling with papier-mâché readily lends itself to projects in science, geography, dramatics, display and in many areas where modeled, three-dimensional forms are valuable as teaching aids. The availability and low cost of the medium will open new experiences in art to a greater number of pupils in the classroom and in their leisure time at home.

21

CHAPTER FIVE

FIBERBOARD WALL MASKS

To improve the acoustics of a room, the building trades have developed a rather light, soft, easily-handled fiberboard. This material can be sawed, filed and sanded easily and quickly, and takes paint well. Like mashed papier-mâché, this is an inexpensive, readily available, and with no stretch of the imagination, a practical art medium. The idea of expressing one's self through this flexible, easily-handled material is not difficult to grasp.

This acoustical material comes in convenient pieces nine inches wide, thirty inches long and one-half inch thick. We found this size was easy to handle on the drawing tables and was also convenient to store. This material can be stored the long way up and down, on its side, or flat, one piece on top of the other, depending upon the availability of storage space. Of course, acoustical and other insulation boards come in various sizes and shapes and under many different trade names.

The acoustical material we used came in packages and it was observed that each end of each package was protected by a plain, unpainted piece of fiberboard. These unfinished pieces had some advantages over the finished, painted boards. First of all, they were not used by the workmen and could be obtained for the asking. Secondly, we could use them at their full length and not as scraps as would be the case of the finished boards which were used by the workmen. Thirdly, these pieces were available as soon as each package was broken. Uniform pieces make it easier to lay out your project. In actually working with the material it was found that painted

fiberboard was not satisfactory to work with in some instances because the paint filled in the crevices of the file and being a harder surface than the surrounding fibers, it could not be shaped uniformly.

Because the material is easy to cut and shape, it has many possibilities. The most efficient way to get added thickness would be simply to glue several pieces together and then cut out the desired shapes and forms. It was discovered, however, that the glue when dry is much harder than the material and poses a problem when it comes to cutting, carving and sanding. Someone came up with an excellent suggestion—why not plan your work out carefully, cut out the desired shapes—each layer of fiberboard would be a different size and shape, carefully cut, filed and sanded and when placed one on top of the other would produce the desired completed design. The pieces, when closely checked to see that they fitted together, could be glued in place. The pieces can be held together temporarily with regular straight pins inserted into the fiberboard at a slight angle. This was a splendid suggestion and has many advantages.

Visualize in your mind or through a series of small sketches what your final design is going to be. Some original sketches may be seen on pages 24 and 25. Remember to take the thickness of your mask into consideration. Next, take a sheet of paper large enough to cover the entire mask, fold in half and draw half of your mask on it. With a pair of scissors, cut along the outline of the folded paper as shown in Figure I on page 28. Open it up and you will have the largest pattern of your mask finished. Place this pattern on the one-half inch thick fiberboard and with a soft pencil, chalk or crayon, trace completely around the pattern. See Photograph I on page 28. If your fiberboard is too narrow, you may glue two pieces together. With a coarse-tooth coping saw cut off roughly any parts of the fiberboard that are too far away from your outline, so as to allow you to use your coping saw without interference as shown in Photograph II on page 28. You may find that in order to use your coping saw effectively you will have to turn the blade to the side. Nearly all coping saws have an adjusting device for this purpose.

Now you are ready to cut along your outline. Choose a convenient place to start cutting, place the saw next to the fiberboard and cut with an even up and down motion. It is not necessary to press forward too hard, let the saw do the work of biting and cutting into the material. Your board can be held in place on the table top, flat side down, with your left hand as you operate with the right hand or vice-versa. With a little experience you will be able to coordinate the movements of your left and right hand in order to facilitate your work.

Your first "layer" is now completely cut out. Next, try to visualize what your second layer will look like as you build up the thickness of your mask. As before, take a sheet of paper, fold and draw your next "layer." This and each additional layer will be smaller than the preceding one. Cut with scissors and trace on fiberboard. With coping saw, rough out edge and cut along outlines.

After the second layer of the mask is cut out, you will probably be ready to cut out the smaller parts and detail such as the eyes, nose, ears, etc. Paper patterns are made for all detail parts first. If some unusual shape is needed for the eyes, you will find that you will not get the result you want if you first fold the paper, so draw it out on a piece of flat paper.

There is a tendency among beginners to make features too complicated or over-elaborate. It must be kept in mind that simplicity is one of the keynotes of good design. Small, complex shapes have poor carrying power; that is, it is difficult to appreciate them at a distance, and since your mask is going to be viewed at some distance when it is hanging on the wall, this is worthwhile to take into consideration. Not only are simple forms more desirable, but forms which cast deep, clean-cut shadows or subtle ones, are most interesting. It is the cast shadows of the various parts of the mask which create fascinating psychological effects. The shapes should be so designed that they cast unusual and interesting shadows no matter from which angle or direction the light is focused.

After you have sketched out the features and details on a piece of paper, cut with a pair of scissors and trace the pattern on the fiberboard. For small parts, use up the scraps of fiberboard which were left over when you roughed-out the large parts of the mask. Now proceed to cut out the parts. A vise might be helpful to hold the small pieces while you are cutting with the coping saw although it is not necessary in most instances.

Assuming that all the parts of your mask are cut out, clean up all the small bits of scrap material and fiber dust. This includes all parts of the mask, tools, floor and all work areas. When working with this material it is necessary to clean up frequently as the fiber dust is light and fluffy and is easily blown about, even with a slight breeze. When cleaning up, save all the paper patterns as you might need them again.

After cleaning up, pick up your first layer. This is the one which forms the back of your mask and is the largest piece. About four or five inches from the top of the mask, drill or punch out two holes about half an inch from each side of the center line. See Photograph III on page 28. The holes need to be large enough to allow a piece of twine to be forced through. This twine should be tied to form a small hoop which is used to support your mask on the wall. Do this now!

Now, place the largest layer of your mask flat on the table and arrange all the rest of your layers of fiberboard, one on top of the other, in organized fashion, and finally arrange the small details. Check carefully to see that your whole mask shapes up and is symmetrical. If you have made any serious mistakes in cutting, check against your pattern. If you are not satisfied with the pattern, then change the pattern and cut

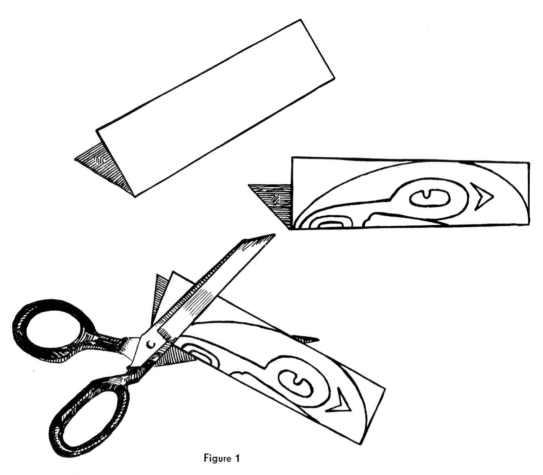

Figure 1

Photograph I

Photograph II

Photograph III

Photograph IV

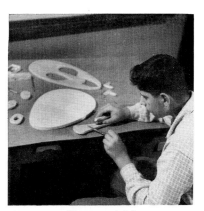

Photograph V

Photograph VI

Photograph VII

29

out another shape from your fiberboard. Arrange with the other parts of the mask and get another view of the total mask.

At this point of making the mask you begin to appreciate the idea of working with individual pieces. This method makes the making of the mask very flexible, saves time and work. Imagine carving the mask in a solid mass and making a mistake!

Assuming that you are now satisfied with the way your parts all fit together to make an interesting whole mask, your next steps are concerned primarily with refinement of the parts as shown in Photograph IV on page 29. This can be accomplished with files and sandpaper, or sandpaper alone, beginning with very coarse and ending up with fine sandpaper. Work around the parts carefully, shaping them to conform with all other shapes. When shaping and finishing the mask, keep in mind the whole mask. You will notice how much easier it is to finish the individual pieces than it would be if you had to carve and finish the mask from one solid piece of material.

If you are satisfied with the shape and finish of your mask, and have checked closely to see if all parts fit accurately, assemble your mask, starting with the first layer placed flat on the table top. Next, using straight pins, secure the second layer to the first and so on until all the parts are temporarily fastened together. Dust the mask carefully and hang it on the wall and begin experimenting with different angles and direction of light to see if you are satisfied with your results. In experimenting with lighting effects you may use an extension cord or searchlight, or if you do not have either of these, hang your mask on each of the four walls of a room in turn and experiment under natural and artificial lighting. Take plenty of time for this, for it is a lot of fun and interesting work.

When checking the mask for interesting shadow effects it is advisable to carry a piece of soft chalk to mark parts of the mask which you might wish to sand or file to sharpen up or soften some of the shadows. It may be even desirable to change some of the small details to improve the mask, so make a note of this, too. Rearranging the features produces different moods and expressions on the mask. Do not fail to take out the pins which hold the features in place and start this exciting adventure of maneuvering the pieces, trying to capture an unusual mood or expression. Linger along with this fascinating game and play it for all it is worth. When you have captured the expression you want, "freeze" it by setting your straight pins firmly and with a soft pencil carefully make an outline by going around each of the features. Your outline will appear on the layer of fiberboard on which you have pinned the features. Do the same for all parts.

Now, take your mask apart, sand or file any parts which require this attention, dust, and begin thinking in terms of gluing the mask together. Any good wood glue is satisfactory for this project. Using a stick or other straight edge as shown in Photograph V on page 29, spread a thin layer of glue on the bottom of each of your cutouts except the first and largest one, and allow the parts to dry. This usually does not take too long for most of the glue is absorbed by this soft, absorbent material. When they are dry, turn the pieces over, right side up and, with a brush, carefully apply glue to the areas which you outlined in soft pencil, which show the location of the parts, coming within one-eighth of an inch of the outline. When all the parts are thoroughly dry, apply another thin coat of glue to the first large cutout which is lying flat on the table top. Place another thin coat of glue to the back of the second layer, lay the part correctly on the first and set the straight pins into it to hold it in place. See Photograph VI on page 29. Repeat the same operation for all the parts and features and let dry for a day or more. When dry, if any dried glue appears along the edges, carefully scrape it off and sand the entire mask with fine sandpaper, dust it and clean up all work areas and the floor. Photograph VII on page 29 shows a mask completely assembled, cleaned up and ready for shellacking.

Next, get some fresh shellac, either white or orange. Remember that any shellac that has been standing around more than six months is not fresh and will not dry well, having a tendency to be sticky. Shellac your mask twice, allowing about one day between shellacking. This will waterproof your mask and give it a hard surface, as otherwise it could be easily dented.

Finally, when it is dry, sand the shellacked mask to a smooth finish and paint it with either show-card or oil colors. Two coats are usually necessary. Sand with a very fine sandpaper between coats.

You can paint your mask many different colors but a bone-white or an off-white tint of one color will prove to be most effective. The mask shown on page 22 is finished in bone-white with the use of wood-filler. If you wish to have a more elaborate finish, try gold- or silver-leaf as a climax to this adventure.

soon back came the animal friends with
good news. They had found a little house
that would be just right.

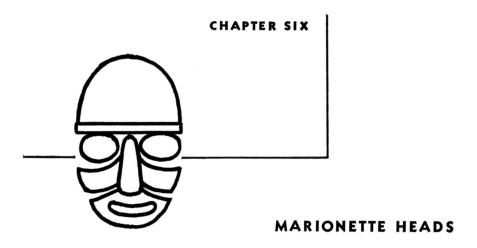

CHAPTER SIX

MARIONETTE HEADS

Marionettes and puppets have a long and fascinating historical background and many famous names through history are linked in some way or another with marionettes and puppets. Archimedes, Plato, Shakespeare, Hans Christian Andersen, George Bernard Shaw, Gordon Craig, Tony Sarg and Edgar Bergen are a few, so you see you are already in excellent company.

To start off with our head-hunting, we decided to experiment with a very resilient material called plasticine. Many marionette makers use the scale of four inches to one foot in making a marionette. This led us to conclude that the head and part of the neck should be approximately four inches.

To begin, take a supply of plasticine and start forming an egg as shown in Photograph I on page 36. This is the basic shape of a head. Knead the plasticine so that your egg shape is compact and solid.

Inscribe a horizontal line with a stick to show where the eyes are to be placed. Half-way between the horizontal eye-line and the bottom of your egg, or chin, is the location for the tip of the nose, so inscribe another horizontal line. If you would divide the distance between the tip of the nose and the chin into three equal parts, you would place the lips one-third of the distance from the tip of the nose. Inscribe another horizontal line for this location. The ears are located between, and touch the horizontal lines for the eyes and the nose. All your horizontal lines are now completed as shown in Figure 1 on page 36.

Now for the vertical lines which are diagrammed in Figure 2 on page 36. Let's begin with the eyes. The width of the eye is approximately the same as the width of the nose or the space between the two eyes. You may inscribe four short vertical lines to indicate the three equal divisions for the two eyes and the space between them. The width of the nose is already determined by the space between the eyes, so bring those two lines down to the horizontal line which is the location for the tip of the nose. The width of the mouth is the same as the distance between the eye pupils or the center of each eye.

Using an orange stick, spoon handle, nail file or a professional modeling tool, gouge out the sockets into which you are going to place the eyeballs. See Figure 3 on page 36. Use the vertical and horizontal lines as guides. Make the sockets about three-eighths of an inch deep. The plasticine which you have removed to form the sockets can now be lumped together, elongated, and used to form the nose. Press this piece of plasticine in the area designated by the inscribed guide lines and with your index finger and thumb, squeeze the plasticine carefully, starting near the eye sockets, and begin to "block in" the nose. Work downward toward the tip of the nose.

Now take two small pieces of plasticine and form them into little footballs. The size of your little footballs will be determined more or less by the size of the sockets. Place the footballs into the sockets and block in the eyes. Work for roundness and fullness, especially in the area just below the eyebrows as in Figure 4 on page 37.

Make two more footballs and press them down a little to make them appear a little deflated. Place one deflated football under the nose and the other above the chin and lo and behold, you have "roughed in" the lips which will look something like the ones in Figure 4. Place your index finger and thumb closely together, about one-eighth of an inch apart, and place them on the upper lip while holding the head in the palm of your other hand. Now, so to speak, start to wiggle your index finger and thumb under the nose—this is a ticklish situation—and start forming the nostrils. After you have penetrated about a quarter of an inch or so, press outward slightly.

Using an orange stick or a professional modeling tool, place the tool where normally the opening of the mouth would be and press gently upward to begin forming the upper lip. Keep in mind that the upper lip is a surface which faces downward at an angle and, so to speak, forms the underside of the area under the nose. If you find that the upper lip lacks fullness, you may find that you may have to add a little more plasticine; if it is too full, simply remove some. Now concentrate on the lower lip. Think of the lower lip as a protruding part and again work for fullness and roundness. Press out a little hollow under the lower lip and add just a little bit of plasticine to give the chin some fullness. Coming back to the lips again, with an orange stick, push up the corners of the lips to begin giving some facial expression. With the head gently resting in the palm of your hand, start turning the head around slowly to check again how the head is shaping up. Check especially to see that your face is symmetrical. If you did something to one side of the face, you must do a similar thing to the other side. When this stage is completed, your head should resemble the one in Figure 5 on page 37.

Next, decide on building up a neck. You will observe that the neck is almost as wide as the head and begins at the base of the ears. If you make the neck from the chin down about a third of the length of the head, and round the end, that will be fine!

Photograph I

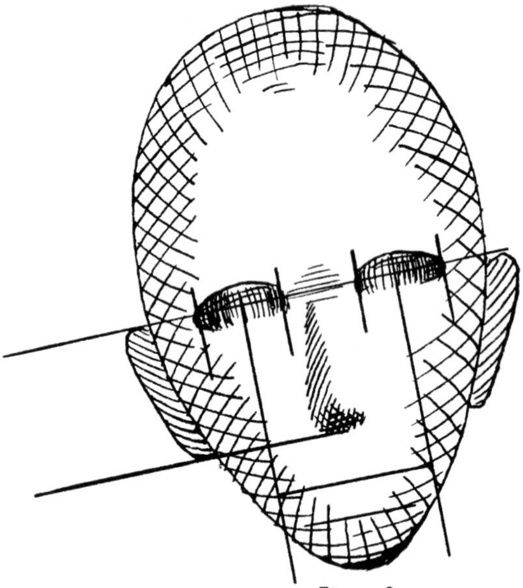

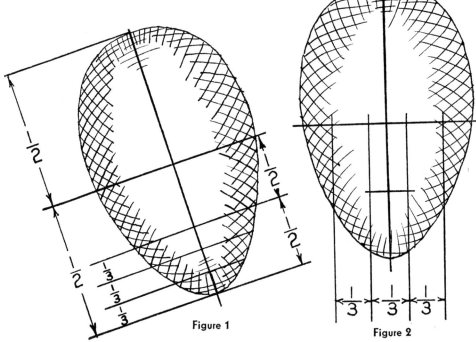

Figure 3

Figure 1

Figure 2

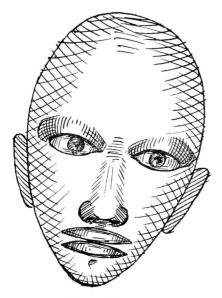

Figure 4

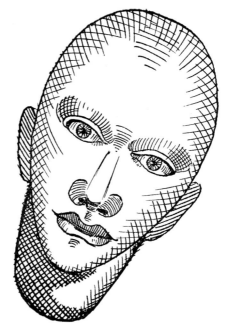

Figure 5

Photograph I shows the basic shape of the head. Figures 1 through 5 show the steps in the development of the head. Photograph II shows the working in of the finer details of the marionette head.

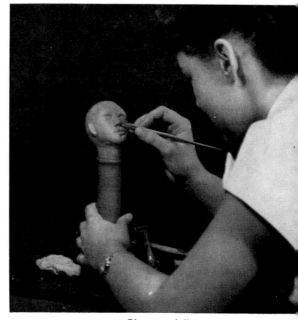

Photograph II

Having completed your head and neck up to this stage, you may place the neck into a milk bottle or a small glass to hold it in place while you begin carefully to work in the details as shown in Photograph II on page 37. A small piece of bent wire or a toothpick are excellent tools with which you can shape, refine and accentuate the features.

No sooner was the experiment in making marionette heads out of plasticine completed, when one boy simply stated: "When are we going to put it into production?" This set the wheels of imagination turning and someone "popped up" with the idea of a "basic" head to save time, space and work. In short, we were to invent a way in which we could turn out a large number of heads in a material that could be worked easily and which would allow the pupils to remove or add on to the material in order to create the characters they wished.

One pupil brought in a bottle of liquid rubber which comes under various trade names. This is an exciting material to work with. Using an ordinary brush, you simply cover an object with about four or five coats of liquid rubber, allowing it to dry between coats. Add a little more liquid rubber to form the base and allow this milk-white substance to "cure." When thoroughly dry it will turn a light yellow. For best results, follow the manufacturer's instructions since many of these commercial products vary somewhat. When this substance is dry, it is as elastic as rubber and can be slipped off the object, turned inside out and cleaned, if necessary. If reinforced with a plaster mold it can be used more effectively.

In order to make a "basic" head from our plasticine one, we mounted the head on a holder. The holder was made by piercing a large nail through a three-by-three inch board, as can be seen in Photograph III on page 40. The plasticine head was, so to speak, impaled with the neck touching the three-by-three inch base. See Figure 6 on page 40. In order to preserve some of the details which might otherwise be lost in the handling, the head was given two coats of shellac with twenty-four hours' drying period between coats. Next, the liquid rubber was applied in much the same manner as described above and shown in Figure 7 on page 40. When the liquid rubber became "cured" and turned a yellowish color, we removed the head from the base and placed it in a paper box approximately five inches wide, six inches long and five inches deep. The head was so arranged and supported that there was half an inch space between the widest point of the rubber-encased head and the paper box. To support the head and allow for a half-inch space between it and the bottom of the box, we improvised a simple wire cradle on which the head rested and it looked similar to Figure 8 on page 41.

Next, we mixed small amounts of plaster of Paris with water until we made a light batter which flowed easily, and then poured it, a little at a time, into the box and over the rubber-encased head. With a pencil we poked and stirred the plaster of Paris to make sure that all the creases were filled and no air holes were present in the mixture. Later, some more of the mixture was made and the process repeated.

After allowing the plaster to dry overnight, we drew a center line along the side of the paper box and took a regular carpenter's crosscut saw and cut right through the paper box, plaster, rubber mold and plasticine head—what an execution! See Figure 9 on page 41.

With the two halves of the plaster cast separated, remove half of the plasticine head, together with the rubber mold. You will observe that the rubber mold is easily removed from the plaster mold or support. The reason is quite obvious for all the crevices and undercuts of the convex and concave forms of the plasticine head have been filled in by the liquid rubber, leaving the outside of the rubber mold, which is against the plaster cast, quite even and smooth. The details of the original, however, are preserved, as shown in Photograph IV on page 41.

And now, let's put the mold to test. Using this mold permits you to make a hollow head. The question now arises, from what to make the shell? Some pupils experimented with a plastic wood filler which comes ready-mixed in convenient, small tin cans. If you pry open the can and feel the mixture, you will find that it is moist and pliable. Another characteristic of plastic wood filler is that it sets rather quickly so it is advisable to handle the mixture with wet hands. Place the rubber molds back into the plaster molds and remove about a cubic inch of plastic wood from the can. With wet hands, pat and press the lump of plastic wood until it resembles a pancake. The thickness of the pancake should be about a quarter of an inch. Insert this pancake into one of the rubber molds and, with your thumb, press firmly and carefully to make sure that all the small crevices will be filled with this material. Wet your hands again and pick up another lump of this material, make another pancake and continue to line the entire mold, overlapping each pancake as you work. When you have completed lining the entire mold the shell should be a little under a quarter of an inch at the top of the head and getting thicker toward the neck. The neck is made solid, thus permitting you to screw an eyescrew into it when the head is completed. The purpose of the eyescrew is to attach the head to the body. A completed head, attached to a marionette body in this manner is shown on pages 32 and 33.

Take a straight edge and gently tap it all around the edges of the plastic wood in your molds to make them straight and level. Allow your mold to dry overnight. In removing the head from the plaster mold you will appreciate the use of a rubber mold, for you will experience no difficulty in the operation. Now peel off the rubber mold from the plastic wood, and you will have a pleasant surprise for the rubber mold slips off very easily.

If you carried out your work carefully, you will notice that the details of the original head are all there despite all the handling. Put your rubber mold back into the plaster mold and you are ready to cast some more heads as the need arises. This

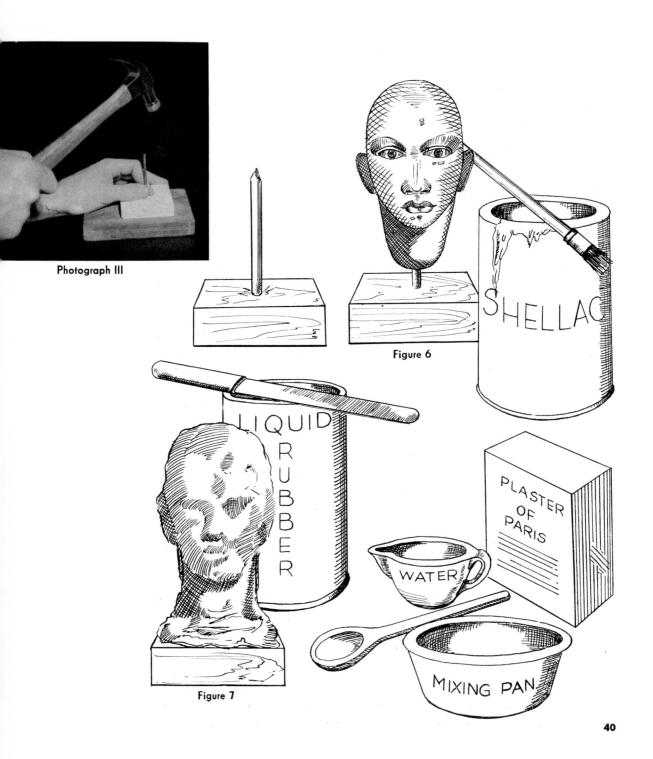

Photograph III

Figure 6

Figure 7

SHELLAC

LIQUID RUBBER

WATER

PLASTER OF PARIS

MIXING PAN

40

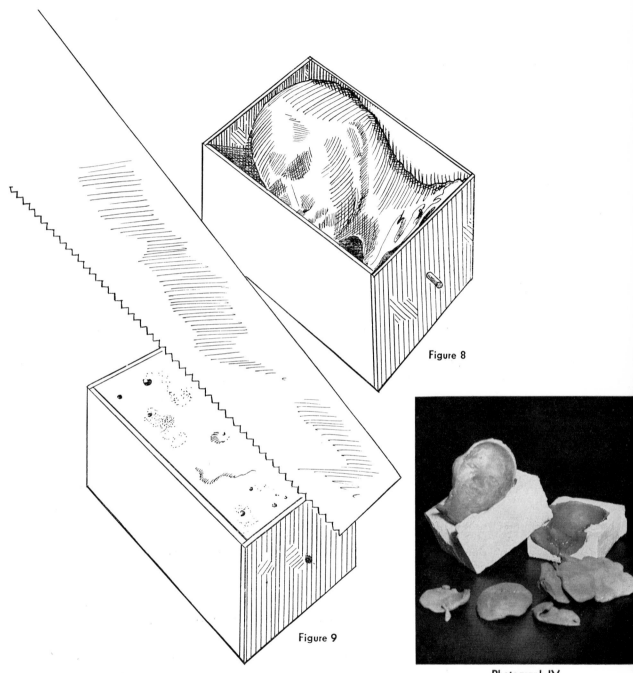

Figure 8

Figure 9

Photograph IV

mold may be used successfully for many years. It stands up well under normal use and needs no special attention to preserve it.

The two halves of the head may now be fastened together with any good quality model-airplane glue. A few rubber bands around the head will help to keep the two halves securely together until the glue sets. When the glue is dry, remove the rubber bands and sand around the seam. If any openings appear along the seam, take a small amount of plastic wood and after wetting your finger tips, force it into the openings. Wet your thumb and run it completely around the entire seam, spreading and smoothing out the plastic wood. This completes your "basic" head.

Some pupils experimented with other materials. One of the boys soaked some newspapers and made a mash by adding wheat paste and developed a shell from it which was very light and durable. Another boy took the soaked newspapers and instead of adding the wheat paste, he put in an approximately equal amount of wood filler. The results were excellent.

After the basic heads were cast, the pupils experimented in changing the features. Linoleum-block carving tools proved most useful for this work. When the basic heads were reshaped, they were carefully smoothed out by sanding the whole head carefully. When this was completed, the eyescrew was screwed into the bottom of the neck and a piece of string was tied to it. Using a soft, half-inch brush, we painted the heads with oil colors, as shown in Photograph V on page 43.

Some children like grotesque heads, others like to give a kind of impressionistic characterization of the head and still others strive for realism. Several types can be seen in Photograph VI on page 43. Figure 10 on page 43 shows the use of a head on the body of a puppet.

Some of the pupils decided to make wigs for their heads. These were made from crepe paper, frayed rope, yarn, excelsior, cotton and numerous other kinds of materials. Best results in making the wig were obtained by gluing a layer of the selected material with model-airplane glue, around the middle of the head and then another layer above this. The wig was then built up in a manner similar to the way shingles are placed on a roof.

One of the pupils decided to experiment with some beeswax which we had in the storeroom, for at sometime or another he had seen an exhibition of figures made of wax and was impressed with the realistic, flesh-like qualities of wax. He used a large metal container, about four inches deep with an opening of approximately five inches. When the wax was heated and in a liquid state the marionette head was held by the string tied to the eyescrew and was slowly dipped into the hot wax and then slowly withdrawn, allowing the hot wax to run off the head with only a thin layer remaining. The thin layer of wax gives the head an excellent life-like appearance and at the same time gives a protective covering which repels moisture and prevents the colors from getting dirty.

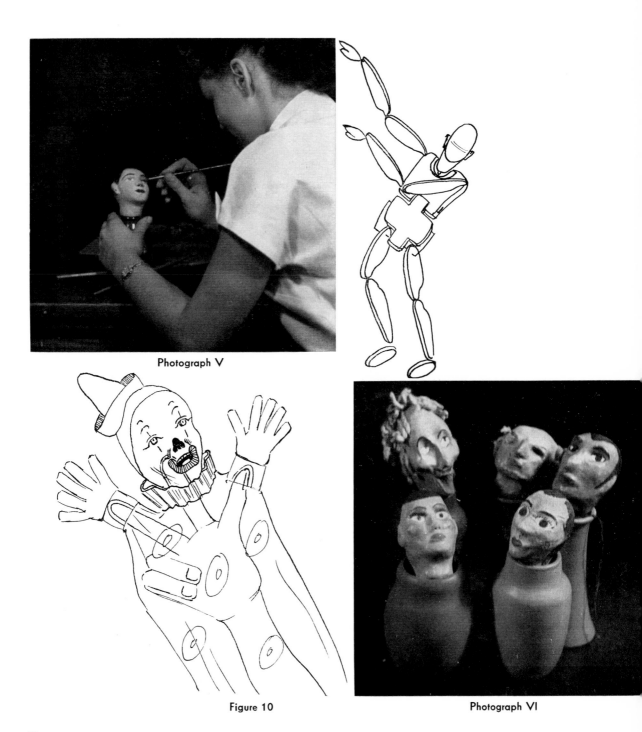

Photograph V

Figure 10

Photograph VI

43

CHAPTER SEVEN

FIBERBOARD THREE-DIMENSIONAL FORM

We all know that the basic head has to take the shape of an egg because all heads are shaped that way, more or less, even though some people, in a malicious way, are called "flathead," "squarehead," "cueball," and the like. This was not of so much concern to us as was what is an average head and where to find one.

Some attempts were made by the pupils to measure their heads with large calipers and dividers and they would then compare notes—something was always wrong with the other fellow's head. "You must have been dropped on the head when you were a baby," became a pet saying. No two people had the identical size of head, but that did not worry me too much as long as in the process of measuring they did not find a misplaced, two-headed individual. Much to the surprise of many boys it was discovered that some of the "swell-headed" girls' heads were actually smaller in size than the boys'. Later it was discovered that most girls' heads were smaller than boys'. Was that the reason why so many boys are "smart alecks"? One difficult thing for the boys to explain to the girls was why so many more girls than boys were on the honor roll in high school. It did not take long to discover that the size of the head had very little to do with intelligence. Not being able to find the size for an average head, we decided to check up with a professional mask maker as to what he considered as "average."

In his book entitled, "Masks," Wladyslaw T. Benda gives the following measurements:

45

SIZES AND PROPORTIONS OF HUMAN HEADS[1]

	Men	Women
From eyebrows to tip of chin	6 inches	$5\frac{1}{8}$ inches
From apex of occiput to tip of chin	$10\frac{3}{4}$ inches	$9\frac{3}{4}$ inches
Width through temples	$6\frac{3}{4}$ inches	$5\frac{3}{4}$ inches
Width of jaws	$5\frac{7}{8}$ inches	$4\frac{3}{4}$ inches

Since Mr. Benda does not use a base over which he shapes his masks, but uses a direct method of working with paper, these measurements represent the outside measurements of a finished mask. Mr. Benda does not adhere to these measurements strictly for he points out that various racial characteristics also affect the proportions of the head and must be taken into account.

In developing and constructing a basic head we used Mr. Benda's measurements as a guide. Thinking in terms of a basic head to get the approximate proportions of the head to save material and time were not the only aspects of the problem. We were also interested in getting the location and size of the features, and in this way we could also save time in diagramming the head. Thus, most of the time could be spent in working to create different characters and types without being bogged down by technical details.

The first phase of mask making begins with sketching the profile of a male head as shown in Photograph I on page 48. We began with a large egg shape and checked the proportions against the measurements Mr. Benda suggested. In making the basic head we decided to develop a three-quarter head because from this a face mask, which covers only the face, and a half-mask, which covers only the upper part of the face, including the nose, could be made. See Figure 1 on page 48 for some idea of the various types of masks which can be made.

When the proportions of the head were checked, we drew the profile, making the indentation of the ridge of the nose mid-way between the top of the head and the chin. The distance between the chin and the nose was divided into three equal parts and the profile of the lip structure was sketched one-third of the distance from the nose. The shape of the chin was then drawn in carefully. Next we followed along with our pencil where normally the jawbone structure is evident; then, just above the ear where the hairline begins. We continued sketching by following the hairline all around the back of the head to approximately where the spine and skull meet.

Next we drew another egg or elliptical shape for the front view, the same length as the profile, and from our measurements obtained the width of the male head. We then diagrammed the elliptical by drawing light vertical lines to locate the center of

---

[1] "Masks," by Wladyslaw T. Benda—Watson-Guptill Publications, Inc.

the head, the width of the nose, distance between the eyes, and width of the mouth. To complete diagramming the head we sketched in the horizontal lines. Mid-way between the top of the head and the chin we drew a horizontal line for the eyes. Half-way between the eyes and the chin we located the tip of the nose. As in the profile view, the distance between the tip of the nose and the chin was divided into three equal parts, and the first third below the nose became the location for the mouth. If you were working alone on these two views, you could draw both of them on a large sheet of paper and with a T-square, simply extend the lines from one view to the next as shown in Figure 2 on page 48.

After having located the guide lines, we drew in the features very carefully. This enabled the pupils to get a better understanding of the shape and relation of the features to one another. See Figure 3 on page 48. With a round-nib No. 1 pen we outlined the drawings with India ink because we believed that in the handling of the work sheet, much of the detail would be rubbed off if left in pencil. Using a hard colored pencil and ruler, we divided the two drawings into one-half inch divisions and drew horizontal lines completely across both views. Now, using a different colored pencil, we drew a vertical center line through the middle of the front view and a vertical line about two inches from the jaw line. This diagramming can be seen in Figure 4 on page 48. This division of the two views into half-inch spaces represented the layers of fiberboard.

Short vertical lines were drawn at each end of the horizontal lines to indicate the exact width of each board. This is an important step, for it might affect the final contours of your basic head. Start from the middle horizontal line and work upward. Connect the next horizontal above at each end of the view and so work downward in the same way. Now you will have steps which touch the outline of your basic head and lead toward the horizontal center line. Check to see that the vertical planes of the steps are away from, and not touching the outline of your two views. See Figure 4 on page 48. Starting at the top of the head, number each division, beginning with the number 1 on top as in Figure 5 on page 49. This will help you keep track of all your parts in the future.

After all this preliminary work is completed, you are now ready to develop your patterns to be used in cutting out your fiberboard pieces. On page 49 are shown two methods of developing these patterns. Figure 5 shows a mechanical way of developing the top view by projection of the side and front views. Figure 6 shows the use of folded paper, applied to the side view to get the width of each piece of fiberboard. It is a good idea to put a small "F-1" on the pattern to indicate the front of the head and the number of the piece. This will help you later on. The paper is then again folded in half and placed over the front face view. This time only half the width of the head is marked off. Next unfold the paper so that now the paper is only folded once. By

47

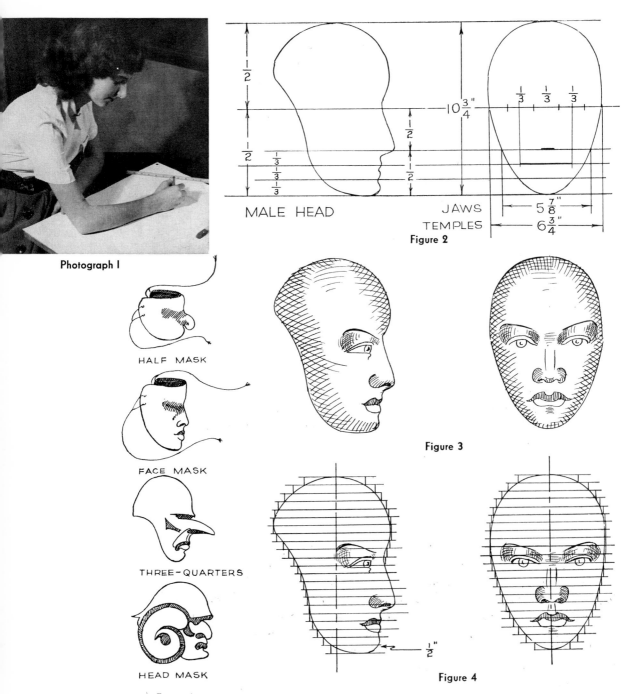

Photograph I

MALE HEAD

$10\frac{3}{4}$"

JAWS $5\frac{7}{8}$"

TEMPLES $6\frac{3}{4}$"

Figure 2

HALF MASK

FACE MASK

THREE-QUARTERS

HEAD MASK

Figure 1

Figure 3

$\frac{1}{2}$"

Figure 4

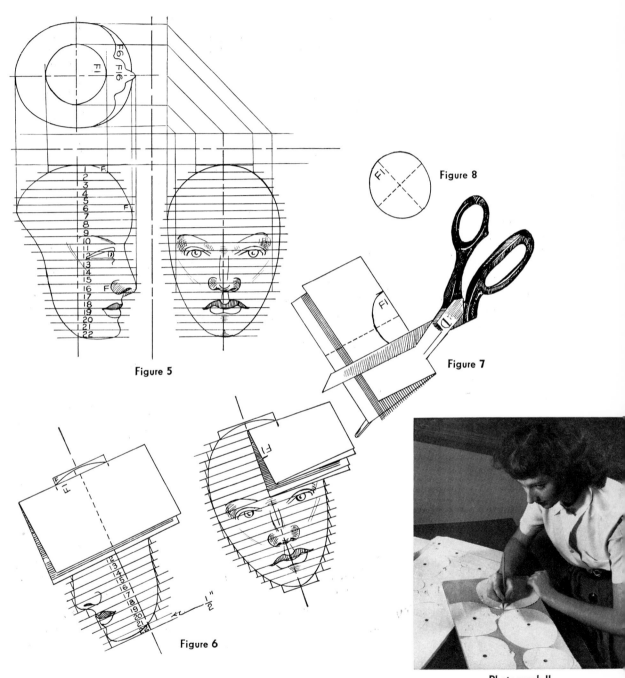

Figure 5

Figure 8

Figure 7

Figure 6

Photograph II

Photograph III

connecting the marks indicating the width and the length of the head, sketch in the elliptical shapes that form the top view of the head.

Now take a pair of scissors and cut around your outline and open it out flat as shown in Figures 7 and 8 on page 49. If it turns out a little different from what you expected, fold the paper again and reshape, if necessary. Do not, however, cut into the pattern beyond the three points which you established. With this setup or pattern of work established, follow this same procedure for each of the numbered pieces.

Assuming that all your patterns are cut out and you are satisfied with your work, bring out the fiberboard. Arrange your patterns on a piece of fiberboard and trace them with a soft pencil so as to get the most economical cuts without placing a hardship upon yourself when it comes to handling your tool effectively. This procedure can be seen in Photograph II on page 49. Next, rough-cut the large areas around the

50

outlines with a coping saw as shown in Photograph III on page 50, and then cut around each individual piece carefully. When cutting out the individual pieces, lay the pieces flat on a table or desk top and press down with your hand to keep each piece in place while you cut with an easy up and down motion. A coarse blade is recommended since fiberboard is a soft material and very little headway would be made with a fine-tooth saw.

After all your pieces are cut, clean up the desk top, tools and floor all around you. Now let's proceed with the next step, which is drilling. Since the pieces which you have cut are still in a rough state, do not attempt to put several layers together in order to drill the vertical center hole. Drill each piece individually by placing the fiberboard piece flat on a scrap board as shown in Photograph III on page 50. Use a half-inch drill for the half-inch dowel as the material is soft and can be forced over the dowel easily, and at the same time this makes for a tight fit. After drilling all the pieces, take a piece of rough sandpaper and smooth out the rough edges of the hole and the contours of each piece. This will help when it comes to assembling the pieces. Clean up all work areas again.

Next, get a piece of one-half inch dowel about fourteen inches long, and a piece of pine board about eight inches by eight inches by two inches. Draw diagonal lines on the pine piece to locate the center and drill a one-half inch hole straight through the center of the board. Using a piece of rough sandpaper, sand the tip of your dowel a little and force it through the center hole by pounding it with a hammer. Your armature is now complete.

Place your armature in the middle of a clean table with your cutout fiberboard pieces next to it. Now take your last piece, the one with the highest number marked on it and hold it in a horizontal position, the right side up and the "F" facing you. Force the piece over the dowel and push it all the way down to the base of the armature. Take the next piece and in consecutive order from the highest to the lowest number force the pieces over the dowel, one next to the other, until you have reached the top of the basic head.

Now align all your pieces and there before you is the complete "roughed-in," sectional, basic head.

After having assembled our pieces and having a "roughed-in" basic head, the next step has to do in the most part with shaping and forming the head. This is done most effectively with a rough, half-round file or some very coarse sandpaper—a wood rasp is excellent. The use of these tools is shown in Photograph IV on page 52. In forming, great care must be taken to keep in mind that the head must be symmetrical. When you have achieved the desired general shape of the head, begin to concentrate on the features which can be easily shaped with sandpaper. As you file, sand and shape, you will soon discover that if you remove some of the pieces of fiberboard from

51

the armature, it will make the modeling very much easier to do. You will begin to appreciate that this kind of setup makes for flexible sculpturing and is most welcome when you begin to model the eyes, mouth and nose.

When you have finished shaping the features, place the layers in their proper place on the armature and check the entire basic head. Make any necessary corrections and finish off with a fine grade of sandpaper. Clean up and dust off the entire work area, tools and equipment.

Now bring out your diagrammatical charts and dividers. Check the entire head and the features very carefully by placing your dividers on the charts, adjust them to the proper distances and then place the dividers on the basic head. Go over the entire head. If there are any discrepancies, mark that area or feature of the head with soft colored chalk. If necessary, you may have to remove some of the layers to improve

Photograph IV

some of the features. Make the necessary corrections, put your head together again and sand the entire head again. Pay particular attention around the features so as not to spoil any of the well-formed parts. Clean up all the work areas and the basic head itself and you are ready for the next step which has to do with gluing and dividing the basic head.

Before gluing the parts of the basic head together, another idea occurred to us to make this basic head in several large sections. This would make it easier to remove the base from the finished paper mask and plasticine which are built up over the basic head. The first step in gluing the basic head into sections is to divide the head into four equal horizontal divisions. Next, remove the layers which form the top section or first quarter of your basic head; then the second large section; then the third, and finally the last section. Apply a thin coat of glue to both sides of each layer of every section except the top and bottom layers of the head. The number 1 piece will be glued only on the bottom side and the last piece will be glued only on the upper side. See Figure 5 on page 49 for numbering. The two sides of the end pieces which form the divisions are not glued.

Allow the glue to dry overnight and when the glue is thoroughly dry, place the bottom piece through the armature and apply a second coat of glue to the top side, taking care not to apply any glue to the armature. If you are making a male head, this would be piece No. 22 as shown in Figure 5 on page 49. Now spread some glue on the underside of the second piece, slide it over the armature and carefully apply glue to the top side of the layer. Repeat this process for each section of the head. Keep in mind not to apply any glue between the divisional layers of the head.

When the four sections of the head are thoroughly dry, turn the head to the profile view and with a soft pencil or colored chalk, draw a vertical line an inch inward from the jaw line. See Figure 9 on page 54. This line is then carried completely around the entire head. Now, using a rat-tail file or a piece of dowel about six inches long, wrapped in coarse sandpaper, sand or file along the line and make a half-round groove about a quarter of an inch deep. When all the sections are complete, a piece of twine or a large rubber band will be put around the head and into the groove to keep the sections in place as can be seen in Photograph VIII on page 56.

Now align the head again on the armature and turn it so that the front view faces you. With a piece of chalk, divide the head by drawing two vertical lines dividing it into three equal parts. Draw these lines up to the fourth or last section as shown in Figure 10 on page 54, and around the head. Hold the basic head firmly with your hand and, with a crosscut saw, start cutting off the first vertical division. Begin at the top of the head and end with the third section. Now cut along the other vertical line in the same way. Your head is now divided into ten separate sections. Sections 2, 5, 8 and 10 are still on the armature.

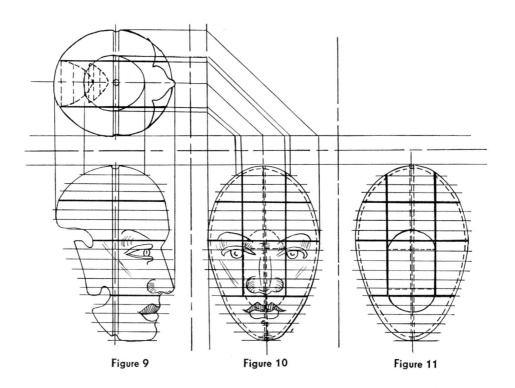

Figure 9   Figure 10   Figure 11

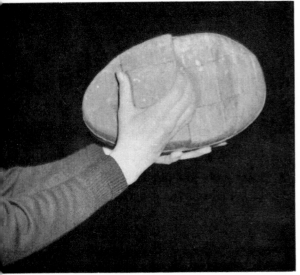

Photograph V

Photograph VI

Remove Section 5 and sand or file off the edge as shown in Figure 11 on page 54. This is to form an opening for your fingers to enable you to pull out Section 8, which is the "king-pin," as shown in Photograph V on page 54. When this center section is removed the basic head collapses. Remove Section 8, and with a rat-tail file or sandpaper wrapped around a piece of dowel, form a groove as shown in Figure 11 on page 54. Finally, remove Section 10 and shape it in the same way as Section 2.

Now dust off all the sections of your head, tools and work area. With fresh shellac and a soft, one-inch brush, shellac all the sections. When the first coat is thoroughly dry, which usually takes about a day, give all the sections another coat of shellac. Treating the basic head in this way waterproofs it and gives it a hard outer protective shell which will make it easier to remove the plasticine when you use it. When the shellac is thoroughly dry, take some beeswax or regular candle-wax and rub a thick coat on the sides of all the sections. Finally, line the sections with aluminum foil.

Now assemble your center sections on the armature. Large rubber bands or a piece of twine securely wrapped around the grooves and tied will hold the outer sections and thus hold your head together. Clean up all work areas and you are now ready to start modeling your head as shown in Photograph VI on page 54. The material which you are going to apply over your basic head when modeling is the same as that used to shape marionette heads as described in a previous chapter. This is an excellent modeling material that does not dry out. It is referred to as plasticine although it is marketed under many different trade names. You will need approximately four pounds of it.

The best tools for modeling are your fingers, an orange stick, hairpin, and some stiff pieces of wire that can be easily shaped to make your own tools as you need them.

Start by applying small bits of plasticine over the entire head. Do not be afraid to experiment with this material. The ease with which this material can be worked makes it possible for you to create many types of characters. The problems of blocking in large areas, locating features, correct size and proportions and other aspects of sculpture are all solved for you. This enables you to concentrate on the features and other parts of the mask which give expression or create a mood, feeling or type.

Finishing and refining of the features can

Photograph VII

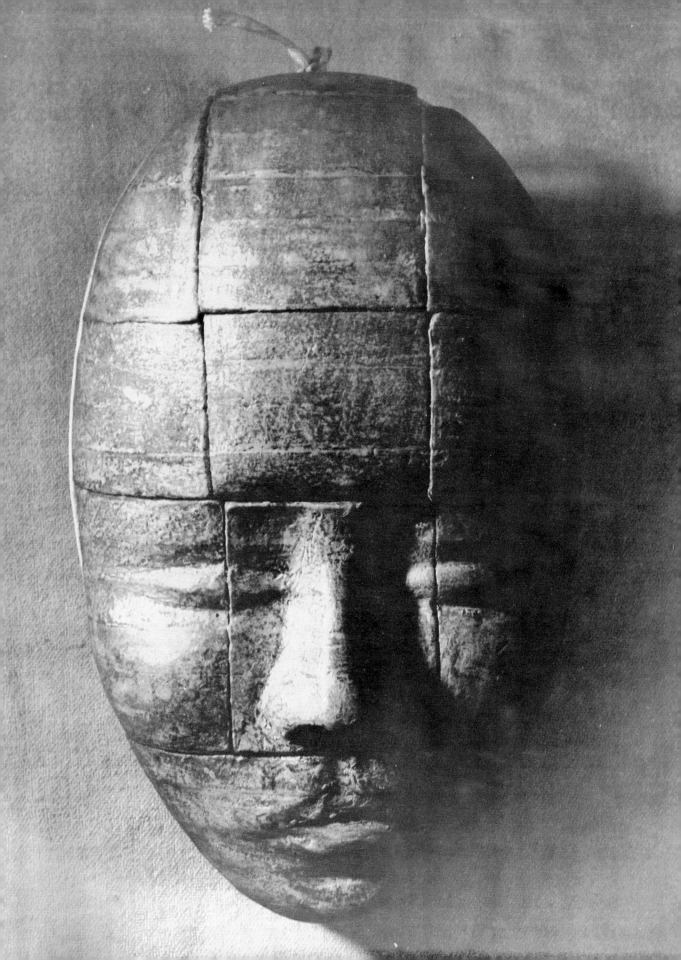

Pasting paper over clay model

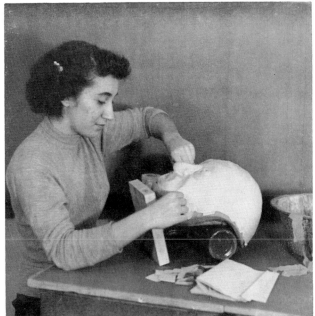

Photograph IX

Reinforcing edge of mask with wire

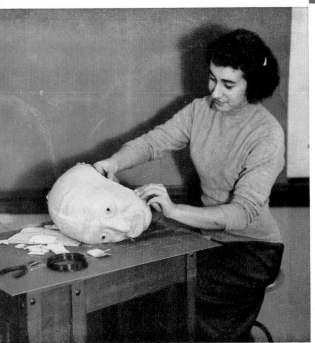

Photograph X

be done with a hairpin, the pointed wooden end of a water-color brush, an orange stick, or sometimes a toothpick can be used effectively. If a real smooth finish is desired, moisten your finger tips in water or use a small water-color brush and very carefully go over all the features and planes of the head.

Now place your head in a direct light and carefully observe the shadows as the instructor and pupil are doing in Photograph VII on page 55. If the features appear to be flat, it will be necessary for you to give them more roundness and fullness through careful modeling. Sometimes it will be necessary for you to add small bits of clay, and at other times it might be necessary to remove some. It is a good idea to accentuate some of the features and make them more pronounced, in view of the fact that some of the detail will be lost when you apply paper over the plasticine.

After the modeling has been completed, check

carefully and you are now ready to begin working on the mask itself. The mask can be made from almost any kind of paper that may be found around the house or school. The paper we found most satisfactory included toilet tissue of many kinds such as "Kleenex," paper hand toweling, newspaper, grocery bags and many others. Before you begin the actual work, it is a good idea to place a newspaper or an old plastic tablecloth under your work.

Now take some soft toilet tissues and tear them up into pieces of various irregular sizes ranging from one-half inch square to about two inches square. Do not cut the pieces of paper with scissors as this leaves a sharp edge whereas tearing the tissues leaves an irregular, "feathered" edge. The feathered edge holds better when pasted together and blends together more evenly with the other pieces.

Your first layer of paper should be soft and very pliable so that it can be easily forced into the detailed parts of your mask. Now, with your fingers, spread a thin coating of regular school paste on one of the small, irregular pieces of tissue and apply it smoothly to the head. Pick up another piece, put paste on it and apply to the head, overlapping the first piece of tissue. Keep pasting until the entire head is completely covered. You will notice that you may have to tear some tissues in different shapes to facilitate pasting with better conformity to some of the shapes of the features. Usually you will find that detail areas will require smaller pieces of tissue and large, simple areas can be effectively covered with large pieces.

A pointed orange stick will prove to be most helpful to force the soft tissues gently into the small crevices and detailed parts. A water-color brush dipped in water may be used to smooth out the paper and bring out the details between the eyes and the bridge of the nose, the nostrils and the upper and lower lips. As you emphasize these details with an orange stick, take care not to puncture through the tissues. It is a good idea to allow the first layer to dry thoroughly after you have covered the entire head before you give any thought to applying the next layer of paper.

When this first layer is dry, tear up some paper hand toweling. This paper is much thicker than the tissue, is tough, elastic when damp and dries hard and smooth. Apply these bits of paper in a similar manner as you applied the tissue. Photograph IX on page 57 shows the application of these bits of paper. When handling the larger areas of the head such as the top of the head, side of the face and bottom of the chin, you will find that you can make your mask stronger if you tear the paper toweling into strips about a half-inch wide and about six inches long and overlay these strips as you paste. When you apply the next layer of paper you can crisscross it by pasting the paper in the opposite direction of the first layer. A finished mask requires about four layers of paper with an extra layer over the top of the head, sides of the face and bottom of the chin, to add strength. It is suggested that you allow each layer of paper to dry thoroughly before applying the next layer. Another important thing to remember is to apply and spread your paste evenly and only on one side of the paper. Press it down firmly so as to eliminate all air pockets. With the exception of the first layer of tissue which is worked quite wet, all other layers of paper should be on the dry side. Enough paste should be applied, however, to assure good adhesion. When paper dries it shrinks considerably and the mask is subjected to rather severe stresses and strains when the drying takes place. If the mask is worked too wet and the whole head is not completely covered with paper, the results may not be too satisfactory for your mask may be distorted.

When the pasting of paper is completed and your mask is thoroughly dry, take some fine sandpaper, smooth out the mask very carefully and dust it off. You are now ready to remove the mask from your modeled, plasticine head.

Place your left hand on top of the molded head and grip the base of the head securely with the tips of your fingers. With the thumb and fingers of your right hand, grip the "king-pin." This is Section 8 of the base head. With both hands, pull and wiggle out the center piece. If you have any difficulty in pulling out this piece, insert a table knife into the openings formed by the sections and work it all around. After you have separated the sections you will find that it will be much easier to remove the "king-pin." Once this "king-pin" is removed, the other sections of the base head can be easily collapsed toward the center and removed. Be especially careful when removing the sections so as not to break the paper mask which is only a thin shell.

After the sections have been carefully removed, take your orange stick and a piece of bent wire and carefully remove any plasticine which may be left on the inside of the mask. When this is done, remove all the plasticine from each of the individual sections of the base head. Put the plasticine away and clean up the entire work area.

The next step is the reinforcing of the mask with wire as shown in Photograph X on page 57. Before this is done, it will be necessary for you to trim the edges of your mask; this is done best with a pair of scissors. Now secure a piece of brass wire, approximately one-sixteenth of an inch thick. The piece of wire should be long enough to go completely around the edges of your entire mask. When you have shaped the wire so that it conforms with the edges of your mask, tear up pieces of paper toweling, approximately one-half inch wide and an inch long. Place the wire exactly against the edge of your mask and paste one of the pieces of paper, first on the outside of the mask, stretch it gently over the wire, guiding it against the edge, and finally paste the paper to the inside of the mask. Repeat this procedure with the next piece of paper, at the same time overlapping the first piece of paper about one-sixteenth of an inch or so.

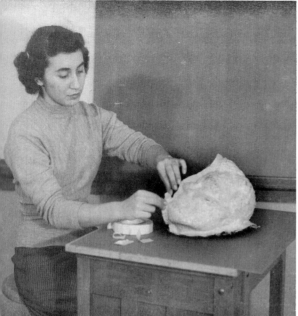

Forming a ridge with masking tape over the rubber mold to divide the head into two halves

Photograph XI

Applying plaster on either side of the ridge. Plaster mold is used to reinforce rubber mold

Photograph XII

60

Applying bits of paper to inside of rubber mold. Plaster mold on outside enables person to press paper firmly against rubber mold

Photograph XIII

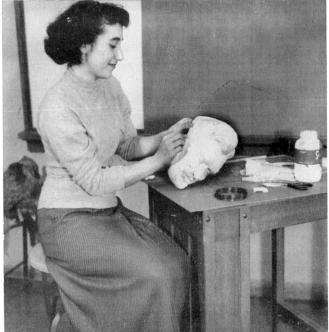

Photograph XIV

Plaster mold is first removed and rubber mold is then peeled off when mask is dry. Final stage in construction is reinforcing edge of mask with wire

When the wire is securely pasted in place and the paper dry, gently sand the area near the edge of the mask to smooth it out. Do not, however, sand over the wire because you might break through the paper and you would then have to paste that part over again. Now clean up the entire work area and spread some newspapers out on the table.

With a good quality, fresh shellac and a soft three-quarter inch brush, shellac the entire mask, inside and out. Allow the mask to dry out thoroughly overnight, and the next day apply another coat of shellac. This will waterproof and help to strengthen the entire mask. When the mask is thoroughly dry, sand with a fine grade of sandpaper, if necessary, and clean up the mask and all work areas.

You are now ready to paint your mask. Your role as a mask maker is a dual one—first, that of a sculptor and now a painter. Use the best grade of permanent oil colors to paint your mask and apply several thin coats, allowing time for thorough drying of each coat. It may take two or three coats of paint before the desired effect is obtained.

A finished, painted mask is shown in the photograph on page 44. For further instructions and details concerning painting the mask, it is suggested that you read the chapter about marionette heads.

From experience gained with marionette heads, many pupils became interested in utilizing similar materials in further developing mask making more along production lines. It did not take long before one of the pupils visualized pouring liquid rubber over the sculptured head, making a supporting plaster cast and, instead of cutting the head in two as in the case of the marionette heads, simply removing the "king-pin" from the basic head.

This idea had many advantages. Whereas some of the fine modeling was lost when the mask was covered with paper, this could be prevented if you had a rubber mold. All the fine details would be on the outside rather than on the inside. Secondly, you could make as many of the same mask as you wanted.

This excellent idea was followed through in much the same way as the marionette head was, and proved to be very successful. Instead of using wood filler, we pasted small bits of paper inside of the rubber mold in much the same manner as pasting paper over the outside of the plasticine head. The big difference, however, was that in this case we developed the mask from the inside out. The steps involved in this development may be seen in Photographs XI and XII on page 60 and in Photographs XIII and XIV on page 61.

On page 63, Photograph XV shows a mask made through the application of bits of paper over the plasticine head and Photograph XVI shows a mask made through the use of the rubber mold technique which is fully described in the chapter about marionette heads.

Photograph XV

Mask made through application of bits of paper over
plasticine head

Mask made through use of rubber mold technique

Photograph XVI

63

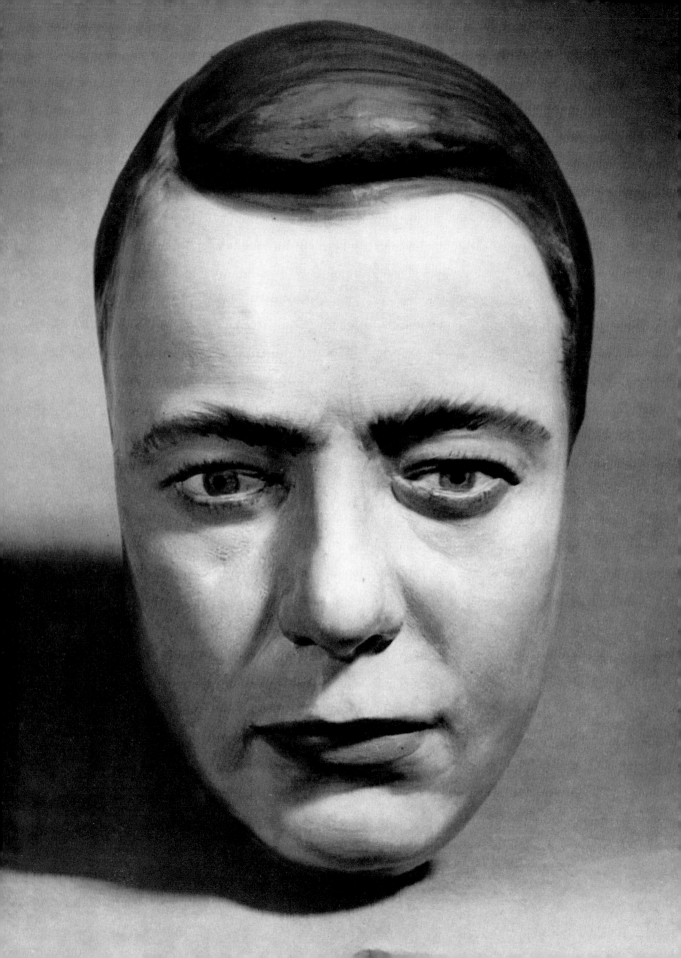

CHAPTER EIGHT

USE YOUR HEAD!

Very realistic portrait masks, reminiscent of wax museums as evidenced in the photograph on Page 64, can be made by making an impression of one's face by using plaster-impregnated bandages. (Medical and surgical supply houses can supply you with this material, called Pariscraft.) Within recent years, experimentation with this material has placed it in a craft category and some art supply houses* now carry it under various trade names.

The use of this material for mask making was explored several years ago when a sympathetic medic gave the author a roll of it which he had left over after he got through winding it around the author's fractured ankle to form a cast.

Plaster-impregnated bandages may be obtained in convenient two inch width and three yards in length. The setting or hardening time of these bandages varies; an extra-fast setting bandage will require two to four minutes and is the ideal kind to use. Other materials and tools which will be needed to make the plaster mold include a pair of scissors, vaseline or cold cream, a small receptacle such as a cup, a mirror, tweezers, paper napkins and some newspapers. Photograph 1 on Page 66 shows some of the materials and equipment necessary.

Making impressions of a person's face has been tried in many different ways, the most common being to lay a person on his back, stick straws in his nostrils and apply plaster of Paris on the greased face. This method is not only dangerous, but because of the weight of the plaster, a correct impression cannot be obtained. The convex facial forms which give life to the face are flattened down so that it is small wonder that impressions made this way are sometimes referred to as a "death mask."

*J. L. Hammett, Union, N. J.; Lyons, N. Y.; Kendall Sq., Cambridge, Mass.; Practical Drawing Co., Box 5388, Dallas, Texas; St. Paul Book & Stationery Co., Corner Sixth & Cedar, St. Paul 1, Minnesota; H. S. Crocker Co., Inc., 720 Mission St., San Francisco 1, California.

65

Photograph I

The advantage of the plaster of Paris bandage is that small pieces of it, approximately one inch square, can be moistened and gently applied to the face to follow the natural facial forms without depressing them. This is also a do-it-yourself method, since a person can apply the bandage to his own face. In the photograph below we see two children in the lower grades applying the bandage to their faces. One child is showing her completed plaster mold while the other is concentrating on making hers.

And now, off to work.

It is a good idea to unroll your bandage and cut it in approximately one inch squares before you begin the application of the bandage to your face. It is well to cut a supply of one-half inch squares for detailed areas around the eyes, mouth and nostrils as well as several longer pieces, approximately one inch by three inches to be used to reinforce the outer edges of the cast. For a sturdy cast you will need approximately a roll and a half of the bandage.

Photograph II

After brushing your hair away from your face, applying some cold cream and tucking a paper napkin under your chin, you are ready to begin.

As an added comfort to yourself, use warm water in the cup into which you will dip the pieces of plaster bandage.

Another advantage of this technique is that a person does not have to be in a horizontal position but can sit comfortably in a chair and work leisurely, guided by his reflection in the mirror.

Start applying the large strips of plaster of Paris bandage to the large planes of the face after dipping the strips in warm water and blotting the surplus water on a piece of newspaper. As previously mentioned, it takes about two to four minutes for the bandage to dry, and since each piece of bandage is individually moistened there is no need to hurry. Apply each moistened piece gently to the face, making sure it conforms smoothly to the facial planes. Make sure that there are no small air pockets. The smoother the strips are worked, the better the impression because the tiny particles of plaster are gently forced through the bandage against the skin.

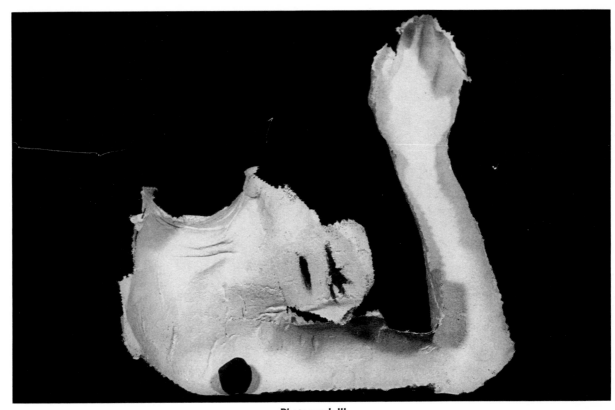

Photograph III

When applying the strips, make sure you get sufficient overlap. Two layers of plaster bandage strips with a third layer around the edges will make for a light, sturdy mold. With a little care you can work around and into the nostrils without impairing your breathing. Tweezers may be helpful when working around the eyes.

Allow approximately five to ten minutes for the mold to dry on the face, then start moving your facial muscles at the same time as you pull at the mold by placing your hands along the edge of the cast, approximately where the ears are located. Without too much effort the mold will be released from the face.

After washing your face, you are now ready to resume work on the plaster mold. Excess vaseline or cold cream may be removed with facial tissue. If you applied your strips of plaster bandage smoothly, the complete mold should be smooth on the inside. If any air holes are visible, or if there are any undesirable creases, these may be filled in with modeling clay or plasticene. A very fine grade of sand-paper may be used to sand and smooth out the inside of the mold.

Photograph III on Page 67 shows part of an arm and shoulder mold to illustrate that large as well as small molds can be successfully made. The complete human body can be taped with plaster bandages and the mold cut into appropriate size sections with an electrical surgical saw. The whole body can be cast in plaster, cement or laminated with paper or fiberglass.

With the rapid growth of the use of fiberglass, several excellent releasing compounds under various trade names may be obtained. Some of them are water-soluble and because of the convenience of cleaning, these are recommended. The releasing compound or liquid is sprayed or brushed on the inside of the mold. After it has sufficiently dried out, according to the manufacturer's instructions, a little high quality floor wax may be rubbed into the mold and carefully polished with a soft rag.

An impression from the mold can be made of laminated paper or fiberglass. For a person not thoroughly acquainted with fiberglass, laminated paper is recommended. If you decide on the paper, you may use paper towels, bogus paper or brown wrapping paper. Softer papers are easier to work with since they are more pliable. Tear the paper into squares of approximately one-half inch and one inch and several pieces one inch by three inches. Apply regular school paste to the strips of paper, make sure you have rubbed the paste well into the paper and apply into the mold. For small facial planes use the small squares; the largest pieces of paper may be used for the outer edges of the mask. Overlap the pieces as you work. If you have used the releasing liquid, you may paste your strips directly to the mold. If you did not use the releasing liquid, place the first layer of paper with the pasted side of the paper strips away from the mold. The second layer may be pasted with the pasted side against the first layer of paper. Usually three or four layers of paper will make for a sturdy mask.

After the mask has dried overnight, remove it from the mold. This will not be too difficult, for the paper contracts a little as it dries and practically loosens itself. Next, trim the outer edges of the mask with a pair of scissors, making sure that it is symmetrical. When this is completed, bend a piece of stove wire along the edge of the mask. The wire is bound securely to the edge of the mask with strips of paper approximately one-half inch by one inch. Apply paste to these strips and place one half of the strip to one side of the mask, then over the wire and paste the other half of the strip to the other side of the mask. Pull down on the strip of paper to press the wire close to the edge. Apply the next strip of paper in the same way, overlapping it approximately a quarter of an inch. Continue in this manner until you have gone around the mask. Where the two ends of the wire meet, overlap them approximately a half-inch and fasten in place with the paper strips.

When dry, sand the mask with rough, medium and then with fine sandpaper. Dust and shellac the inside and outside of the mask. Then again sand with fine sandpaper and prime the mask with a good grade of oil base paint. After drying, sand again with fine sandpaper and paint the desired skin, eye and hair colors. Look into a mirror and study the color carefully and paint it realistically if you are making a self-portrait.

If you plan to work with fiberglass, visit a boat supply house where you can buy the supplies in small kits. A great deal of care must be used in sanding and smoothing the inside of the mold with particular attention paid to details around the eyes, nose and mouth.

After the releasing liquid has been applied and is dry, mix the resins by following the instructions of the manufacturer for the required hardening time. Add the flesh-colored pigment to the resin mixture. This preparation is sometimes referred to as the gel coat and may be applied with a brush over the releasing compound. To hasten drying an electric light bulb may be used. Brushes should be washed with acetone.

The next day, mix some clear resin and after lining the gel coat with a thin layer of fiberglass matting, dip a one inch wide paintbrush into the resin and dab the resin over the fiberglass without stretching the fiberglass matting. After four to six hours apply another layer of fiberglass matting and more resin. Three or four layers will suffice. When dry, remove from mold; trim the edge of the mask with a hacksaw and sand the edge.

Prime the mask with a special fiberglass primer and complete painting the details with a high quality oil base paint.

A word of caution—a fiberglass mask takes a great deal of skill to make and requires considerable experience to get excellent results. However, the time and effort to develop this skill are well worth it for fiberglass is a fire resistant material of great strength, durability and beauty.

69

CHAPTER NINE

PAPER FORM—VERTICAL AND HORIZONTAL PLANES

The more you work with masks, the more you begin to visualize the face in different terms. Some think of the face in terms of planes, surfaces and areas; others think of the mask in terms of a shell or thin covering over the face. Still others start by thinking about the anatomy or structural aspects of the mask. One of the pupils thought about masks in terms of boat construction. He began to think about placing cutout vertical frames, with slots, in predetermined openings along a horizontal plane or base. Let's follow this procedure, step by step, and see how this idea was developed.

The materials which you will use are easily obtainable in school or around your home, and include about eight sheets of nine- by twelve-inch drawing paper and about five sheets of nine- by twelve-inch cardboard; old display cards, tortion board, illustration board or any other stiff paper will do. Tear into about one-inch squares enough wrapping paper, paper napkins, paper towels or any other paper that can be easily crumpled, to fill a cigar box. Regular school paste, wallpaper-hanger's wheat paste or a handful of regular kitchen flour mixed with water will do. Secure a light wire coat hanger or a piece of baling wire or any other wire that bends easily but retains its shape. The wire, in most cases, should be a little over two and one-half feet in length.

The tools with which you will work are as easy to get as the materials, for example: pencil, eraser, a pair of large scissors, a sheet of fine sandpaper, a wood rasp or a sheet of the coarsest sandpaper that you can get. A No. X-24 waterproof carborundum sandpaper is recommended. A single-edge razor blade or a sharp pen-knife will prove helpful.

W. T. Benda, as the result of a lifetime study of the subject, gives the following measurements of an average male head. We have used these measurements and found them very satisfactory. According to this authoritative source, the male head is approximately ten and three-quarters inches from the top of the head to the chin; six and three-quarters inches wide at the temples and five and seven-eighths inches wide at the jaws. The dimensions of an average female head are approximately one inch less than the dimensions of the male head. You will notice that these same dimensions were used for the fiberboard three-dimensional form which is discussed in a previous chapter.

Your first step in the actual construction of the mask after you have your basic idea fairly well established is to draw in pencil on a sheet of nine- by twelve-inch paper, an egg shape to conform with the above-mentioned measurements. Having drawn the egg shape for the head, diagram it as shown in Figure 4 on page 73. Begin by dividing it horizontally in two, this will be the location for the eyes. The length of the eyes is roughly the same as the distance between them, as shown in the diagram. Draw another horizontal line half-way between the line for the eyes and the chin, and you have the location for the nose. The distance between the nose and the chin is then divided into thirds; that upper third gives you the location of the mouth. This is probably all the diagramming you need to help you locate the features and guide you along in an orderly manner.

Working from your sketch, place the features in their approximate locations. After you have developed the front view of your mask, take another sheet of nine- by twelve-inch drawing paper, draw another similar egg-shaped form and begin working on the profile. By placing one sheet next to the other, you can get the proper location for the features by projecting lines from your front view. After you have carefully drawn your profile view, draw a vertical line through your drawing, approximately where the jaw ends and the ear begins. This will give you a full-face mask.

Next, cut out both the front and profile views of your mask and trace on stiff cardboard and cut out again. At the high points of the chin, nose and forehead, cut out slots about one inch long and one-sixteenth of an inch wide. These slots can be seen in Figure 6 on page 73, marked 1, 2, 3.

Draw a vertical center line on the front view, as shown in Figure 4 on page 73, and along this line place the straight end of your profile view. Take scotch tape and fasten the cardboards together. The profile view is now perpendicular to the front view.

This accomplished, fold a sheet of nine- by twelve-inch drawing paper in half. Place the folded end of your paper in an upright position along the side of the profile view on the slot at the high point of the chin. Using your sketches, study out the shape of your chin and begin to draw a cross-sectional view on the folded sheet, starting at the top of the profile and working downward and toward the outside edge of the front view. Now, about an inch and one-half below the chin line, draw another similar line. In addition, it will be necessary to cut out a slot to correspond with the slot in the profile view. With a pair of scissors, cut out this form; open and lay flat on a piece of cardboard, trace and cut out. It will then look like Figure 1 on page 73. This done, make a similar form to be placed over the slot at the nose. Here again, your sketches and front view will help you determine the width of the nose. This form is shown in Figure 2 on page 73. The form for the forehead is also made in a similar manner and resembles Figure 3 on page 73. Press each form down in place and with some scotch tape fasten each end to the front view. When all the forms are in place, the structure will be similar to the structure being assembled in Photograph I on page 74.

Using another nine- by twelve-inch drawing paper (if you are making a male head you will need a slightly larger paper) fold in half and draw a large half-pattern to conform with the contours of the front view of the face. Locate where the eyes and mouth should be and draw a large oval socket for the eyes and a large oval opening for the mouth. Leave a thin strip of paper about one-quarter of an inch, along the folded edge, which will later be placed along the profile of the nose. Using a pair of scissors, cut into the fold along the one-quarter inch strip and around the eye socket. Start again where you first cut into the folded line and begin cutting the opposite way and end up by cutting out the large oval opening for the mouth. In addition, three slots are cut, one in the center of the forehead and the other two at the temples. Open this pattern and lay it out flat. It will now look like the pattern in Figure 5 on page 73. Place the pattern over the cardboard structure which you completed and fasten it along the edges. Next, fasten the one-quarter inch strip along the profile of the nose and lips. This is shown in Photograph II on page 74. When you come to this stage, your project will resemble a human skull. The two sockets for the eyes and the two openings for the mouth and nose are the most important areas in which you can develop and show expression in your mask.

Now is the time to get your paste and cigar box full of bits of paper and begin forming the nose with these bits of paper to which you have applied paste, either with a brush or your finger tips. These bits of paper may be torn or cut into any desired shape to facilitate the forming of the features. Care must be taken to press these bits of paper together tightly as you build up your mask. The forming of the eyes and lips cannot be done hurriedly and requires considerable attention and care. When you have covered the entire face with these pasted bits of paper as shown in Photograph III on page 75, and the mask has thoroughly dried, take the rasp or rough sandpaper and go over the entire face, sanding all the rough spots and shaping out the details of the features. Where radical surgery is necessary, do not hesitate to use a single-edge razor blade. If you cut, file or sand through the mask, do not worry for you can easily patch it up. From here on, it is a process of repeatedly building up with bits of paper, filing, cutting and sanding until the desired results are obtained. When your mask reaches this stage, remove it from the form; then tear out all the loose bits of paper from the inside of the mask. Scrape and sand out the inside of the mask. If any breaks occur, patch them up with bits of pasted paper again. When finished, your mask should be about one-sixteenth of an inch in thickness.

The final step in constructing your mask is to bend a lightweight coat hanger or other stiff wire to conform with the outside edges of your mask. With a piece of fine wire or transparent scotch tape, bind the edges of the wire together. Place the wire along the edge of the mask and with small bits of folded paper, paste the wire to the mask.

When your mask is sanded smooth and all the bits of paper are securely and firmly pasted down, hold the mask against a strong light bulb and check for any weak

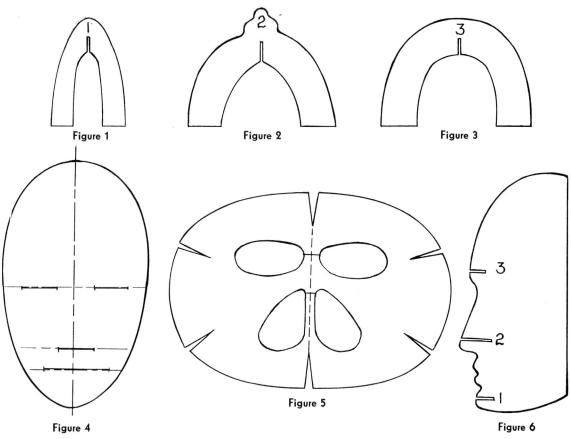

Figure 1   Figure 2   Figure 3

Figure 5

Figure 4   Figure 6

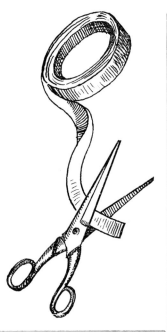

Photograph I

Assembling the vertical and horizontal planes to form cardboard structure

Attaching the paper pattern over the cardboard structure

Photograph II

Photograph III

Pasting bits of paper over paper pattern

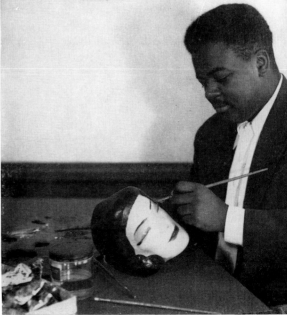

After filing, cutting, sanding, reinforcing with wire and shellacking, the mask is painted twice with a good grade of oil colors.

Photograph IV

75

spots. If there are any weak spots, they will probably have to be built up from the inside and sanded lightly again, when dry. You are now ready to give your mask a coat of shellac. Use fresh shellac of the best quality and when dry, sand lightly and shellac again, allowing the mask to dry a day or two before painting.

When painting masks, as the pupil is doing in Photograph IV on page 75, the fact that the skin coloration of human beings varies considerably must be taken into consideration. For example, photograph on page 77 shows a brunette mask; photograph on page 78 is of a monkey face; and photograph on page 79 shows a blonde mask. It goes without saying that different colors and values have been used for each.

You can begin by mixing orange and white and add yellows, browns and purples to get variations. The mask may be painted with good grade oil colors or show-card colors. When using oil colors, rub the color into the mask with your thumb and fingers or use a soft-hair brush. Two coats of paint are usually enough, if you are satisfied with the results. Two more coats of good quality linseed oil will give a finish and a gloss to your mask, if you think this will help it. In many instances we observed that a flat finish gives a more realistic appearance. If you use show-card colors, you may dip the whole mask into beeswax; the result will be a very lifelike effect.

When the above directions are followed carefully, the maker is more than repaid for the time and effort because the result is a thing of beauty with surprising strength, durability and usefulness which, with normal care, will give a lifetime of pleasure and satisfaction. These masks may be used for decorative purposes as well as for functional uses; for example, various assembly programs, television shows, holiday parties, carnivals, contests, plays, all kinds of dances and many other activities too numerous to mention.

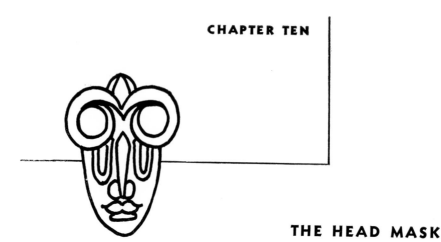

CHAPTER TEN

THE HEAD MASK

In making head masks we thought in terms of human marionettes. When designing a full head mask which is to be used for acting, many factors must be considered. In order to cover all the functional aspects, a list of activities associated with wearing a mask and acting was made. This list included:

1. Size and comfort
2. Breathing
3. Visibility
4. Hearing
5. Ease of putting on and removing
6. Weight and strength of mask
7. Ability to hold in place when moving head from side to side or up and down
8. Storage
9. Ease of keeping clean
10. Wearing qualities

We concluded that the best approach toward making a full head mask was to begin with vertical and horizontal planes as discussed in the preceding chapter. However, instead of covering the head with several paper patterns, we decided to use chicken wire. We discovered that corrugated paper would be an excellent material from which vertical and horizontal planes could be cut. Corrugated boxes can be easily obtained from your neighborhood grocery store, and this paper has many advantages. It can be cut easily with a knife, scissors or razor blade; it is light, strong and rigid; it is strong enough to allow you to model over it with chicken wire, yet it can be crushed or crumbled with no difficulty and removed when mask is completed.

When drawing the horizontal and vertical planes we referred to the measurements of the male and female heads mentioned in Chapters IV and VI. These measurements were increased one inch all around to allow for comfort, breathing and ease of handling.

Photograph I on page 82 shows the stage of assembling the corrugated vertical and horizontal planes. One complete piece was made of the profile of the head, and front view or width of the head. Smaller, arc-shaped planes were cut to conform with the shape of the hairline, forehead, nose and chin. Another large, arc-shaped plane was cut out and placed in back of the head to aid in forming the hair arrangement.

There is no one prescribed way of arranging the various planes since they all differ somewhat, depending on the character portrayed and how each plane can best aid you in further developing the head. Notice how each piece is inserted into another. The idea of cutting slots part-way in two pieces and then putting one piece into another was taken from an egg box.

When the vertical and horizontal planes were put in place, they were fastened to each other with pieces of masking tape about an inch and one-half long. Half of the piece of masking tape was pressed firmly to the end edge of a horizontal plane and then overlapped on either side. The remaining, protruding piece of masking tape was then overlapped tightly over the vertical center plane, thus securing the two planes firmly. Another good idea for fastening the horizontal and vertical planes together was to use a large paper punch and twine. About half an inch from the end edge of the horizontal plane, punch a hole. Square the horizontal and vertical planes and with a pencil draw a line along the end edges of the horizontal plane on the vertical center plane. Next, with your punch, make a hole one-half inch in and away from either line. Thread a piece of twine, about two and one-half inches long, through the three holes and tie securely.

Once you have fastened all your horizontal and vertical planes, either with masking tape or twine, your structural head should look similar to the one shown in Photograph II on page 82. You are now ready to start thinking in terms of chicken wire.

Chicken wire comes in many sizes and can be purchased very reasonably at your corner hardware store. You will need about a square yard for a large full head mask. One-inch mesh was found to be most satisfactory. With a piece of string, measure the distance around the profile, beginning with the chin and ending with the base of the hairline in the back of the head. Now cut several large strips of chicken wire the length of the string and about six inches wide. A pair of large tin snips will do a fine job of cutting the chicken wire. If you do not have this tool, a pair of pliers with a cutting edge may be used.

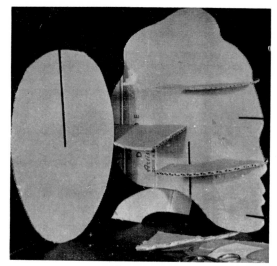

Photograph I

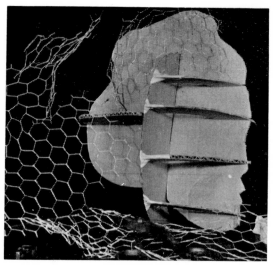

Photograph II

Photograph III

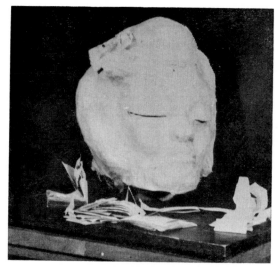

Photograph IV

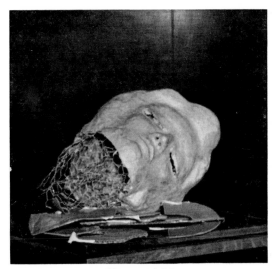

Photograph V

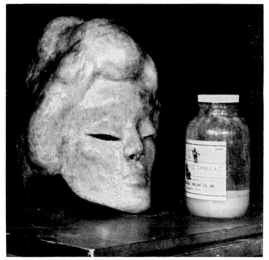

Photograph VI

Photograph VII

Photograph VIII

Take one strip of chicken wire and place it around the edge of the profile and then begin to form the chicken wire by pressing it into the depressions and up and down along the features. When working with this mesh, remember that what you are actually doing is sculpturing with it. By pressing the hexagon shapes of the mesh with your thumb and index finger you can distort them to fit your needs in shaping and developing the features. The better the job you do with sculpturing with wire, the less work you will have when working with paper, later on.

Now take another long strip of wire and shape it along the outside of the other vertical plane that gives you the width of the head. Shape the mesh carefully before you decide to connect this strip with the one that you shaped along the profile view. If you find that there is considerable overlapping of the two strips of chicken wire on top of the head, take your tin snips and cut off the surplus. Start connecting the two strips of wire together. Begin at the top of the head and fasten the strips of mesh evenly all around the head—remember that you are sculpturing with the wire rather than just covering a form. If there are any openings between the strips of mesh, cut narrow pieces of wire and sculpture and fasten them in working around the entire head. Do not complete one section at a time or you may discover to your surprise that something quite unexpected occurred on the side opposite from where you were so earnestly and conscientiously working. When your head is "wire-sculptured" to your satisfaction you are ready for the next phase. Before going on, however, clean up the entire work area. There is always something refreshing about a new, clean start.

The next phase of your work has to do with applying the paper over the wire mesh. Tear strips of paper toweling about one-inch or so wide and about six to eight inches long. Use regular school paste or mix powdered wheat paste and water into a batter. Dip the strips of paper toweling into the batter or paste, remove the surplus and begin to apply the strips over the mesh, beginning with the top of the head. It is a good idea to take the end of your pasted strip and tuck it through one of the openings in the mesh and then paste it under your strip. This will anchor your paper in place. Photograph III on page 82 gives you a cross-section view of a head, showing some of the paper pasted to the mesh.

As you work along pasting and overlapping the strips of paper, keep in mind, just as you did when working with the wire mesh, that you are not just covering the wire mesh with paper. What you are doing is sculpturing with wet strips of paper over the wire mesh. You will discover that it lies to your advantage to work in various directions with the strips of paper to achieve the desired shape and prevent the paper from slipping off the mesh. If you find that the paper does not stay in place in the hollow or convex surfaces, poke your finger through the paper and make a "window" in the wire mesh. With smaller pieces of paper, put a trim around your window, thus holding it securely in place to the wire mesh and patch over it again with a strip of paper. Making the strips of paper behave is a great adventure and a lot of fun. Work all around the head until it is complete. Your first layer of paper is now allowed to dry thoroughly. If weather permits, place the head near an open window. This will facilitate drying and if you have a bad neighbor, this may give him a good scare.

When the first layer of paper is dry, usually overnight, tear up some more strips of paper. It is advisable to get another brand of paper toweling. Check to see that the other brand of toweling is of a different tint. This is the reason for buying it, for it will help you see if you cover the entire head evenly with the second layer of paper. Before applying the second layer of paper, smooth out any rough spots or undesirable shapes caused by the drying of the paper. This can be done with rough sandpaper, scissors or a razor blade.

When applying paste to the second layer of paper, work more on the dry side. This time use school paste and apply the paste to only one side of the strips of paper. Paste the strips of paper over the entire head and pay a little more attention to the features and other details of the head. Photograph IV on page 82 shows this phase of the head completed.

Although you are actually sculpturing with paper, a large amount of modeling and sculpturing is also done when the paper is dry. This is done with a coarse emery paper or a wood rasp. Shape up the second layer of paper with either or both of these tools. Do not be afraid to make a hole through your mask if it is necessary as this can be very easily patched up.

For the third layer of paper, use the brand of paper toweling that you used for the first layer. The different tinted paper will again make it easier for you to distribute the paper evenly over the entire head.

As the mask slowly evolves from a rough to a more finished appearing head, there is a feeling of anxiety and anticipation as the mask maker works toward completion of the head. Seeing the mask grow and change is a fascinating experience. Each change brings with it new challenges which sometimes call for patience, courage, determination, understanding, imagination and many other human characteristics. It is the human experience which makes mask making a great adventure and the finished mask is only one of the accomplishments of this experience. It has one big advantage over other human experiences in that you can actually see it, put your fingers on it and say, "There it is."

At this stage of mask making your imagination and effort should be concentrated on trying to give full play to the character and type of the personality which you are trying to create. Make frequent reference to your sketches and other reference material which you have gathered from the library, art galleries and other sources. Try to give your work fullness and expression that is characteristic of life. Pay particular attention to the features, especially the eyes. When working around the eyes, keep in mind that partly-closed eyes give more expression and sometimes a touch of mystery to the face. Avoid large openings for the eyes; a large opening is a hole, empty and meaningless which, at best, detracts and may even spoil the effect that you are trying to create.

Now, back again to the mask. When the fourth layer of paper has been carefully pasted and shaped around the head, then dried, and the details worked over with sandpaper and rasp, you are ready for the next step. Clean up the entire work area and give yourself plenty of elbow room. This is the time when you are going to "knock the stuffing" out of your mask.

Gently place the head on its side with the chin pointing at you. See Photograph V on page 83. Now place your left hand on top of the head and grip the underside of the hair firmly with your finger tips. With the fingers of your right hand, start crushing and crumbling the first horizontal corrugated plane. Pull out this piece of corrugated paper and work into the inside of the head, removing all the horizontal and vertical paper forms. When this operation is completed, start loosening the wire mesh around the opening, working your way into the inside of the head until the entire wire mesh is divorced from the paper shell. Be careful so that you are not scratched by the wire. Next, compress the wire mesh until it is small enough to be pulled out of the head without damaging the shell. When you have pulled out the wire mesh, remove any loose paper inside of the mask. Then take a piece of coarse sandpaper about three inches square and carefully sand the entire inside of the mask until it is smooth and uniform in thickness. Treat the inside of the head mask with the same affection and care as you do the outside.

After sanding the entire inside of the mask, dust out the head mask by gently tapping on the outside. The vibration will loosen all the dust particles. Now, with small pieces of paper coated on one side with paste, patch up any depressions which were caused by breaks in the mask. Next, line the entire inside of the mask with overlapping pieces of torn paper toweling. When applying the paste to the paper, work on the dry side; this helps to do away with shrinkage. When the inside of the mask is dry, put it over your head to see if the opening is large enough. If the opening is not large enough, cut away some of the mask.

When this is completed, paste up the loose or frayed edges; then paste pieces of paper about one-inch square all around the outside of the mask, letting them protrude about one-half an inch. As you work around the edge, fold the end pieces over to form a ninety-degree angle, thus forming a rim around the opening of the head mask. Build and reinforce this rim from the inside of the mask with small bits of paper. The rim should taper out slightly. When the inside of the mask and the rim are thoroughly dry, trim the rim with a pair of scissors and sand smoothly and evenly all around. Next, get a piece of brass wire about one-sixteenth of an inch thick and shape it around the outer edge of the rim. Apply some paste to small bits of paper toweling, about one-inch square, and paste them around the wire, securing it to the outside and inside of the mask along the outer edge of the rim.

With sandpaper, carefully shape up the features and sand the entire mask, inside and out. Dust the mask and with a finer grade of sandpaper, again sand the entire mask, inside and out. Dust the mask carefully and clean up all work areas.

Using a good grade of fresh shellac and a one-inch brush, shellac the entire mask, inside and out. Allow the mask to dry overnight, and the following day shellac the mask again. When it is completed up to this stage, your mask will be similar to the one shown in Photograph VI on page 83.

Painting the head mask is an important part of mask making and has been discussed to some extent in the chapters dealing with marionette heads and fiberboard three-dimensional forms. When painting the mask, use only the best permanent oil colors. It may be necessary for you to paint your mask three or four times.

After the first coat of paint has been applied and dried as in Photograph VII on page 83, turn the head around slowly and study it from all angles. It may surprise you to discover certain defects in modeling which have been brought out as a result of applying color to the face. Do not hesitate to do a little plastic surgery. With a razor blade and rough sandpaper, sand, scrape or cut out and then apply bits of pasted paper to improve certain planes of the face. Sand the patches carefully so that they blend in with the rest of the face. When you have completed the face-lifting, shellac the patched-up areas and when dry, touch up with paint again. When the painted patches are dry, sand the entire face very lightly with fine sandpaper and dust with a brush or a piece of soft cloth.

You are now ready to paint your mask a second time. It is important to pay considerable attention to mixing and selecting your colors. Color can be effectively used to help bring out the personality and type of your head mask. However, do not think of color in terms of covering up the mistakes of poor modeling and sculpturing. Try to paint the second coat as near to what you want the mask to look like as you can.

Use a soft brush to paint the face with, to do away with sanding when the mask is dry. To achieve texture effects, use a variety of stiff and soft brushes when painting. Pay particular attention when you paint the hairline. Use a stiff, half-inch or three-quarter inch brush and "feather" it in as shown in Photograph VIII on page 83. This will do away with a hard line and will give the softness and texture effect that is associated with natural hair.

When the second coat of paint is dry, place the mask over someone's head and observe the mask at a distance. Have the model go through a series of slow movements and gestures and you will experience an unusual, eerie sensation. A mask in movement is magic indeed. The wearer of the mask will almost be compelled to act or dramatize the role of the personality that the mask depicts. You don't believe it? Well, then, place the mask over your own head, look into a large mirror and you will soon discover that the mask "does" something to you.

Because the mask is somewhat larger than your head, you will discover that it does not set comfortably on your head. It will be necessary for you to make a harness or headband. After several attempts to make a headband, we discovered that the most effective kind was a rim made of fiberboard. With the use of a coping saw, rasp and sandpaper we were able to make it fit snugly into the mask, just a little above eye level. Next we cut the inside out to complete the rim and after using the rasp to smooth out the rough edges, we finished it off with sandpaper, dusted and tried it on for size and comfort.

When it was found that the rim fitted snugly into the mask and around the head of the individual, it was given two coats of shellac. When dry, the rim was pressed firmly inside of the head mask. This rim made the head mask stay firmly and comfortably in place when the head was turned from side to side and up and down. To make sure that the head mask would stay in place if any quick, abrupt motions were made by the wearer, a piece of elastic cord was used. Two brass paper fasteners were inserted into the head mask, approximately in the vicinity of the temples, one on each side of the head. If it was found difficult to insert the brass paper fasteners, small lead holes were pierced through with an awl. Do not attempt to make these lead holes with a knife since the blade of the knife is tapered and as you insert the blade through the mask and press, it is difficult to control the exact amount of penetration. When you have made the holes with an awl, take a piece of elastic cord about one-half inch wide and a foot long and pierce a hole about one-half inch from either end. Now, force the brass fasteners through from the outside of the mask. On the inside of your mask, force the fastener through one end of the elastic where you have punched a hole with an awl or small punch. Spread the ends of the fastener apart, pressing firmly against the mask. The same thing is repeated with the other end of the elastic except that the fastener is not spread out until you have properly adjusted the elastic to fit snugly but not too tightly under your chin. The button of the brass fastener that is exposed on the outside of the mask may be touched up with a little paint to blend in with the color of the hair to make it less conspicuous.

On the following two pages are shown photographs of two of the masks which were made and used in the production of "Aladdin and the Magic Lamp."

CHAPTER ELEVEN

BODY MASKS

Body masks are similar to head masks, the basic difference being the size. Since the body mask is much larger, it usually requires more material and time to make. They seem easier to make than a head mask in some instances, especially if the design of the body mask is kept simple and bold.   Our masks were built on a long table, located in a convenient out-of-the-way place in the back of the room, because we planned from the beginning that this would be a long-range project worked on by different students throughout the day.   In the beginning we were not exactly sure what we were going to make but all agreed that it could be some kind of bird.   Since the body mask had to fit over the human body, we began to think in terms of the functional aspects of the design.   Among other things, we took the following factors into consideration: safety, comfort, weight, circulation of air, visibility, size, color, ease of putting on and taking off, attractiveness, simplicity.

After having conceived the idea and studying the problems involved, the next important phase was to determine just how effectively and economically we could bring this idea to realization.   No reference material or preliminary sketches were used.   Instead, we worked directly with the material, trying to understand it, make it behave, and exploit it to its fullest advantage.   It was decided to select an "average" size pupil around which the mask was to be built.   The pupils seemed to think that a boy approximately five feet, eight inches tall was the answer to the problem.   Heavy baling wire, which can be purchased in almost any hardware store, was used in the preliminary construction of the body mask.   With a piece of baling wire approximately six and one-half feet long we made a hoop and held it in a horizontal position around the middle of the boy's body to see if it fitted comfortably with ample room to move about. The wire circle had an overlap of approximately three or four inches and was bound in place with rubber bands. The reason for the overlap and use of rubber bands was to allow for adjustments and flexibility when shaping the general form of the bird.

This large circle was then held in a vertical position in the middle of the table. Three or four pieces of baling wire, approximately six feet in length, were attached at mid-point to the vertical hoop with rubber bands. The wires were approximately a foot apart along the hoop. Another slightly smaller hoop was formed and attached to the horizontal wires about a foot above the first hoop. Still another hoop approximately the same size was also fastened to the horizontal wires a foot below the first hoop. More hoops were added above and below the first or middle hoop. The further we worked away from the middle hoop, the smaller were the other hoops, with the exception of the head. More vertical wires were added as the body, head and beak took shape. A piece of wire approximately five and one-half feet in length was used to make a hoop, which was fastened with rubber bands mid-way in front of the bird. This was to serve as the main opening for putting on the mask. The drawing on this page gives a somewhat more detailed picture of how the project looked at this phase of construction, referred to by many students as the "bird cage" phase.

After the "bird cage" was completed, a couple of pupils used great care in assisting a third pupil in putting on the wire body. Necessary adjustments and minor

Figure 1
A wire frame, referred to as the "bird cage," was first step

DRAWING BY AUTHOR

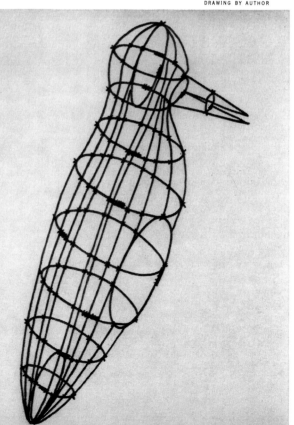

92

changes were then made. It was estimated that about one hundred feet of baling wire was used. The next step was to enclose the "bird cage" with chicken wire.[2] Cut with tin snips into pieces approximately two feet by three feet for convenient handling and shaping. After carefully forming the chicken wire over the cage we fastened the pieces together with string, weaving it in and out.

The bird was now ready to be covered with paper. We used about fifteen pounds of wheat paste, a small bundle of newspapers and about twenty feet of gray felt paper. The felt paper was obtained from a linoleum store. First we mixed the wheat paste in a pail, following the manufacturer's instructions. Next, black and white newspapers were placed on a table and with a wallpaper-hanger's paste brush a liberal amount of paste was applied to the sheets. The sheets of newspaper were then torn into convenient sizes and applied to the chicken wire. After the first layer of black and white newspaper was applied over the entire frame, a second layer of colored or "comic" sheets was applied. It was not necessary to have each layer dry before applying another layer. The black and white and colored newspapers were applied alternately and the body evenly built up. Then the mask was allowed to dry for a couple of days in a well-ventilated room. When dry, the mask was sanded with coarse sandpaper. A layer of felt paper was applied over the entire mask, making sure that all depressions and irregularities were corrected by putting on more paper in the necessary spots. Minor irregularities often occur since the entire mask is under considerable stress and strain when the paper dries.

After the mask had dried for a couple of days, the rubber bands and string inside the mask were cut. The baling wires were carefully removed as well as the chicken wire. The whole mask, both inside and out, was then gone over with a rasp and coarse sandpaper. The edges of the beak were reinforced with baling wire. Pieces of felt paper approximately one inch by two inches were torn, paste applied to them, and placed over the wire and fastened to the mask. The pieces overlapped each other by approximately one-quarter inch. The large opening in the mid-section of the bird was formed like a rim and was reinforced with wire, securely pasted in place in the same manner as mentioned above except that larger pieces of paper were used. A final layer of felt paper was pasted on the inside of the bird. We used regular school paste for this last step in pasting in order to keep the paper more on the dry side, thus avoiding the risk of any distortion caused by the drying of paper. When dry the whole body mask was sanded, inside and out, starting with a coarse grade of sandpaper and gradually working down to a medium grade. The mask was then carefully dusted and cleaned out.

A harness was made from parachute shrouds, although any laundry rope would do as well. Two shrouds were cut, approximately two and one-half feet in length. Two

[2]Approximately fourteen feet of three-foot wide chicken wire was used.

pieces of cardboard, approximately one-half inch by six inches with two holes punched along the center line approximately four inches apart, made up the shoulder straps. These holes were punched with the pointed end of a brush and were large enough to allow the shrouds to pass through easily. Attaching the shrouds to the mask was a simple matter. Four holes, large enough for the shrouds to pass through, were punched approximately mid-way in the back of the bird, two on each side. These holes were approximately six inches from each other along a vertical line. Horizontally, they were about fourteen inches apart. Two holes were also made along the top part of the rim opening, one on each side about fourteen inches apart or each seven inches from an imaginary center line. The shrouds were then knotted at one end and threaded through the holes in the back of the bird. The knot was on the inside of

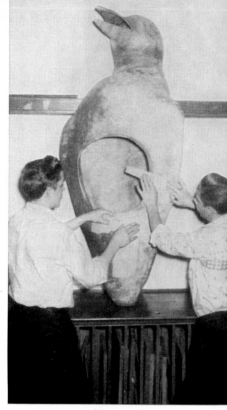

Photograph I
Wire armature covered with chicken wire and then with papier-mâché

Photograph II
Completed body mask modeled by student

PHOTOGRAPHS BY AUTHOR

the bird. Then the shrouds were slipped through the shoulder straps and finally through the holes in front of the bird and knotted. The last knot was on the outside of the bird.

The bird was then given two coats of shellac. The entire mask was sanded with a fine grade of sandpaper after each coat of shellac. One coat of flat white oil paint was then applied. After the paint was dry, the details were sketched in freehand with a piece of charcoal. The mask was then painted with fast-drying enamels. Two coats did a fine job. For drying time of paints it is best to consult the manufacturer's instructions which are given on the paint cans. Although the bird turned out very well, what really was most important was the job of creating and doing and what it meant to the growth and development of the children who were involved in this project.

CHAPTER TWELVE

FIBERGLASS MASKS

New materials bring with them new challenges, techniques, processes and advantages, and so it is with fiberglass, which has been usually associated with boat building. So well has this image been ingrained, that sometimes persons are surprised when they find out that many other original objects can be successfully created with this unusually flexible and versatile material. As a matter of fact, most of the information about the material and techniques used in mask making is the same as used in boat building, the difference being that when working on a mask, we work in miniature, so to speak.

After modeling a face in plasticene, careful attention should be paid to make sure that no unusually pronounced undercuts are evident in the features since these would hamper in making an impression from the mold. Fiberglass is strong enough to allow the impression to be "sprung" away from the mold if the undercut is not too pronounced. A skilled craftsman with experience in handling fiberglass could easily determine the tolerance needed to successfully free the impression from the undercut. The beginner should, however, try to do away with undercuts until he learns more about the limitations and advantages of the material.

The finished product, when it leaves the artist's hand, is called the core. It can be made very smooth or may be textured. When the desired results are achieved, the next step is to apply a Mold Release Agent which can be applied with an airbrush, charcoal drawing atomizer, or brush.

The mold release agent is essential for use in lifting out cast or molded forms. It prevents sticking by providing a thin film between the object and the finished mold. It is fast-drying and usually water soluble. It is always best to follow the manufacturer's instructions.

The mold release agent can be used over objects made of plaster, wood, plastic and other materials. Sometimes it is better to give two coats of mold release agent to make sure that the subject is completely covered. When dry, the next step is to apply the Gel Coat which is the first coat used in making molds. It comes clear and can be pigmented, which means that color can be mixed with the gel coat. It is not necessary to get a specially prepared gel coat, regular polyester resin may be used. When using either clear or pigmented gel coat a catalyst hardener must be added. The

96

amount used will be determined by how soon you wish the resin to set. Polyester is a thermo-setting medium which means that it hardens chemically. Drying can be speeded up by using a heat lamp or placing the object in the sun.

The gel coat or first coat is applied to the mask core with a brush after the hardener has been added and mixed. It is best to work outside in the shade on a windy, dry day. If you work inside, make sure the room is well ventilated and using a fan is very helpful.

It is better to give two light gel coat applications rather than one heavy one. Two coats will assure better coverage and less dripping.

Polyester resin comes in different temperature settings. For example, if you live up north and plan to work in an unheated garage, a low temperature resin is best and can be used in temperatures in the 45° to 55° range.

When making a mold, the gel coat is sometimes pigmented with a specially prepared paint which comes in paste form. It is available in white, black, blue, green, silver, yellow and red and a concentrate of two ounces will be enough for one gallon of gel coat.

After painting on the gel coat with a good quality brush (other than a plastic one), wash the brush out in acetone which can be purchased in quarts or gallons.

For a more permanent mold, epoxy resin is used instead of polyester. It is used in the same manner but costs about twice as much. It is usually used for production molds.

After the gel coat is dry, which could be anywhere from twenty minutes to twelve hours, depending upon how much hardener you used and at what temperature you were working, your next step is to apply fiberglass mat. This comes in various thicknesses and widths but the basic weight is 1½ ounces per square foot and the width is fifty inches. You may save money by purchasing assorted fiberglass remnants accumulated from ends of rolls. Some large companies sell these in ten pound bundles.

The thickness of the fiberglass mat does not matter too much since the layers can be peeled off. Fiberglass mat is made of long, criss-crossed, interlocking fibers, not woven but matted to provide thickness and a high absorption vehicle for resin work. Fiberglass mat is easily worked to make good and detailed impressions.

Tear off pieces of fiberglass matting about three inches square and peel each square into thirds. Get enough peeled squares ready to cover the mask about two times. Experience has shown that a thin, flexible mold is better in most cases than a thick one.

Mix some polyester resin and hardener and apply a liberal coating with a clean brush over the mask, or core, which you prepared with a releasing agent. Next, take one of the squares and place it over the wet resin, starting around the eyes and nose. With your brush moderately saturated with resin, tap the matting against the core in an up and down motion. Do not attempt to brush it on from side to side because this only thins out the matting. Great care should be taken to make sure that all the details are worked in. Apply the next square of matting, and the next, until you have gone around the whole mask. Overlapping gives added strength and assures that the core is completely covered. When you have finished, start to apply the second layer of mat squares. It is not necessary to wait until the first layer is dry. If any air bubbles are detected, they may be pricked with a pin. When finished, wash the brush out in acetone.

Fiberglass comes in many weights, sizes and weaves. The matting gives bulk and is good for capturing details, but by itself it does not have too much strength. If you plan to use your mold several times, it is advisable to reinforce it with strips or squares of four to ten ounce fiberglass fabric.

Just a few words of information about different kinds of fabrics available. There is the matting which has been mentioned, the fine fabric and also woven roving—a coarser weave used for large objects and boats. Also available are tapes used for finishing edges and chopped strands which are used with a blow-gun and spray gun in a production set-up.

Now, back to your mask. Mix enough resin to cover the mask. This is determined by the amount of resin you used for the gel coat and the matting. Add the hardener, stir well and apply liberally over the matting. Apply the cloth in much the same manner as you applied the matting although you will find that a side to side movement may be used with the brush when saturating the cloth with resin. When working on large, flat or slightly curved surfaces a squeegee or roller may be used. One or two layers of cloth will suffice.

It is most important to exert a great deal of care in making the mold since your finished product will be only as good as you make the mold.

After applying one or two layers of fiberglass cloth and the mask core is completely and evenly covered with overlapping pieces of cloth, wash the brush thoroughly with acetone and allow your mold to harden. On damp days the resin will set more slowly and it might be advisable to use a 250-watt infrared heat lamp, reflector type, in any household fixture to hasten hardening.

If all goes well and the mold is hardened, removing it from the mask or core should not be a difficult job. Insert the blade of a table knife between the mold and the core and pry it loose around the edges and soon your mold will "pop off."

Inspect the finished mold carefully for it should be smooth. If any imperfections appear such as pit marks, these will have to be filled in. If the mold has too many imperfections, it is almost a waste of time to sand and patch it up. It would be simpler and better to start all over and make another mold.

You will notice that when you remove the mold the thin film which clings to the mold and the core acted as a separator. A little water will wash the film off.

Should it be necessary to fill in some wrinkles or pit marks in the mold, mix a little Thixotropic powder with resin to make a putty-like mixture, add hardener, mix well and apply over the defects with a spatula and remove all excess material. Don't let the word thixotropic scare you, it is only a fluffy, lightweight, highly refined white powder which comes in half-pound bags.

The putty-like substance which you mixed may be stored for days without hardening until the hardener or catalyst is added.

Inspect your mold again by holding it against bright light to see if there are any weak spots. These may be reinforced with a few strips of cloth. The rough edges of the mold may be smoothed out with a rasp and coarse sandpaper, followed by fine sandpaper. Wash out any remaining film from the inside of the mold with water, dry the mold and you are now on your way to make the impression of a finished fiberglass mask.

Apply a coat of good quality household wax to the interior of your mold. Spray or paint on two coats of releasing agent, the same one you used over the core. When it is dry, apply two coats of wax over the releasing film or agent. Next, prepare more three inch squares of matting and place on the sides of your mold.

The process of making the impression is the same as making the mold. The only difference is that when making the mold you worked on the outside and when making the impression you are working on the inside—a big difference.

Somehow or other the first impression the author made resulted in most of the resin flowing into the nose of the mask. To remedy the situation, thixotropic powder was added to the resin to thicken it and more hardener was added to make the resin set more quickly. After a few experiments a person gets the "knack" of it and some excellent results were obtained.

If the mask will get a lot of use, it may be reinforced with fiberglass cloth. Sometimes it is only necessary to reinforce the outer edge of the mask with cloth.

Photograph I on page 95 shows the mold and impression made of a Balinese mask. No pigment was used in making this mold; however, as mentioned before it may be desirable to do so. The impression was released from the mold by inserting a table knife between the mold and impression just as it was done in releasing the mold from the core.

This photo also shows some of the materials and tools used. The rectangular box with plastic bag showing contains the thixotropic powder. The white gallon plastic jug contains the acetone. The small two ounce jar stores the pigment while the small plastic squeeze bottle and the dark colored bottle both contain hardener.

Looking at the photograph you will also notice that marine resin was used since the marine supply stores are a good source to get fresh supplies because of the fast turnover of products.

The table covering in the photograph is also fiberglass cloth and gives the reader some idea of the size in which it is available. The other materials in the photograph are also fiberglass cloth.

The finished mask was completed with regular oil paints after it had been painted with regular white oil color.

There are already new materials on the market to replace fiberglass cloth such as Dynel with tensile strength per square inch which almost matches steel. Then there is Polypropylene which is a hundred times stronger than fiberglass, ten times as flexible, abrasion resistant, and less expensive. Polypropylene fabric may be used with polyester and epoxy resins.

Join the parade of progress and experiment with mask making with these challenging materials.

APPENDIX

On the following pages are photographs selected from the excellent collection of masks at the Buffalo Museum of Natural Science. This selection was made with the cooperation of Miss Virginia Cummings of the Museum staff. These masks have been selected to give the reader some idea of the variety of materials that have been used by the people throughout the world in making masks. These selected photographs do not, by any means, represent a complete or exhaustive exhibit. In selecting these masks, considerable attention has been given to craftsmanship, attraction, variety and, to some extent, world-wide distribution.

Perhaps the most important reason for including this exhibit is to awaken the reader's imagination and motivate him to invent or create original masks and to experiment with the many new materials of today. It is not the intention of the author to include these masks for the reader to copy or imitate.

To the more scholarly person, the exhibit may serve as a fascinating means of discovering the use and meaning of the masks, or perhaps it will lead him to speculate as to the psychological reasons which make people use such objects.

To the person who is neither scholarly inclined nor interested in making an original mask and perhaps finding new uses for it, it is hoped that this exhibit will serve to acquaint the reader with the masks so that he will gain greater appreciation of them as works of art.

Belgian Congo—Wood

China—Bronze

Bakuba—Cloth and Shells

Belgian Congo—Wood

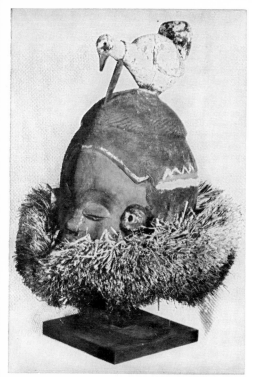

Belgian Congo—Wood

New Ireland—Wood

New Britain—Wood

Iroquois Indian Cornhusk Mask